A must read for all sincere God-seekers—one of the most unique and comprehensive guides to the spiritual life I've seen. In *Journey to God*, author Dan Burke provides an unambiguous compass to the life-giving water we are all thirsting for.

—*Donna-Marie Cooper O'Boyle, EWTN host, speaker, and author of numerous Catholic books including* Rooted in Love: Our Calling as Catholic Women

I count myself among the many who have long needed spiritual direction, but have been unsure regarding who to receive it from or how to get started. Dan Burke's wonderful new book is filled with practical wisdom and sound Church teaching on how to navigate and grow our interior lives. I will be referring to and recommending this gem for the rest of my life. Well done!

—*Randy Hain, senior editor of the* Integrated Catholic Life *e-zine and author of* The Catholic Briefcase: Tools for Integrating Faith and Work *and* Along the Way: Lessons for an Authentic Journey of Faith

It is a special grace to be able to entrust the direction of your soul to someone else, for it is far too easy to get lost on our journey toward God. A good spiritual director can help you retain your interior composure, particularly during times of stagnation, lukewarmness and discouragement. It is a joy to be able to lay bare your most intimate thoughts and feelings with someone who can help you; someone who understands you, supports you and prays for you. With this handbook, Dan has provided a clear map on how to find that person and choose that path. Follow it! It will change your life forever.

—*Terry Polakovic, founder of ENDOW*

In this book, Dan Burke places a compass in our hands—the compass of Christ-centered spiritual direction. I highly recommend this book. He has done a great service for anyone seeking spiritual direction and who desires to deepen their relationship with Christ.

—*Sister Timothy Marie, OCD, Carmelite Sisters of the Most Sacred Heart of Los Angeles*

This book is a persuasive statement of the well-nigh universal need of us Catholics for spiritual direction. It offers a wealth of wisdom regarding preparation for, and proper use of, spiritual direction. It draws heavily and convincingly on the Catholic tradition of mystical theology. Fully a third of the text offers a detailed, helpful guide to spiritual self-examination. Dan Burke offers a very apt analogy for the use of spiritual direction: In traveling the road of spiritual growth, spiritual direction is like a clean windshield, a good rear-view mirror, with side mirrors to help detect blind spots.

—*Rev. Ray Ryland, Ph.D, JD, Columnist for* The Catholic Answer
and Chaplain of the Coming Home Network

A plan is necessary for the success of any endeavor. The spiritual life is no exception. Dan Burke's accessible book provides a framework for anyone seeking to grow in relationship with our Lord. I am amazed at the amount of helpful material that is packed in this modest-sized book. It certainly will help those in the early stages of their spiritual walk and it also will provide perspective for those further along in their spiritual life. As a retreat director, I intend to make this helpful text available to retreatants. In fact, I've already told the publisher that I want to be the first to place an order.

—*Regis J. Flaherty, director of the Gilmary Retreat Center
and author of* God's on the Phone: Stories of Grace in Action

This book is positively rich in "helps" for the person seeking sound spiritual direction, and wanting to learn how to rightly order and cultivate a good interior life. Dan Burke has written the "go-to" guide for any question you have about spiritual direction and making progress in the spiritual life. All the information you need, from a most trustworthy source—I highly recommend it!

—*Sharon Lee Giganti, Catholic Answers speaker and New Age expert*

JOURNEY TO GOD

Journey to God

Daniel Burke

WITH FR. JOHN BARTUNEK, LC, STL

DynamicCatholic.com
Be Bold. Be Catholic.®

JOURNEY TO GOD

©2012 by Dan Burke
Published by Beacon Publishing
with permission from Emmaus Road Publishing

Printed in United States of America [1]

ISBN: 978-1-937509-80-4

Originally published as
NAVIGATING THE INTERIOR LIFE

Cover image: reproduction of a seventeenth century icon featuring St. Basil the Great, St. John Chrysostom, and St. Gregory the Great, Historical Museum in Sanok, Poland. Used with permission.

Nihil Obstat: Colin B. Donovan, S.T.L., Censor Deputatus
Imprimatur: ✝ Robert J. Baker, S.T.D., Bishop of Birmingham

Cover design and interior layout by Claudia Volkman

As she has never failed to do, again today the Church continues to recommend the practice of spiritual direction, not only to all those who wish to follow the Lord up close, but to every Christian who wishes to live responsibly his baptism, that is, the new life in Christ. Everyone, in fact, and in a particular way all those who have received the divine call to a closer following, needs to be supported personally by a sure guide in doctrine and expert in the things of God. A guide can help defend oneself from facile subjectivist interpretations, making available his own supply of knowledge and experiences in following Jesus. [Spiritual direction] is a matter of establishing that same personal relationship that the Lord had with his disciples, that special bond with which he led them, following him, to embrace the will of the Father (cf. Lk. 22:42), that is, to embrace the cross.

—POPE BENEDICT XVI

TABLE OF CONTENTS

FOREWORD

How many times have you opened a book that promised to change your life, only to become disillusioned by the end of it (or long before!) upon finding that you did not understand it or agree with it, or that you simply were not willing to exert the willpower necessary to follow the author's advice on how to lose weight, improve your memory, speed read, or run for office and become the governor of your state?

The book you now hold in your hands is substantially different, but before I tell you why, it might be helpful to share the vantage point from which I offer this observation. By God's mercy and grace, I am a priest of thirty years and have had the great privilege of providing spiritual direction to souls ranging from a supreme court justice nominee, a United States senator, a prominent radio talk show host, priests and women religious of various orders, and good, hardworking lay men and women. From where I stand there is nothing more important than the aggressive pursuit of progress in our relationship with God.

Why? Because death is inevitable. Billions of dollars are spent yearly and endlessly to cure diseases, push back the onset of mortal illness, and—in the case of diehard atheists—attempt to prolong life for thousands of years, anticipating a time when humankind will achieve immortality. Even a former U.S. president said, "I want unlimited scientific discovery and I want unlimited applications. We want to live forever and we are getting there" (William Jefferson Clinton).

But those of us who are sincere practicing Catholics know that our most important work in this life is to prepare ourselves for the next one, where we really will be immortal. That means at a minimum remaining in God's friendship (a state of grace, free of mortal sin). More ambitiously, it means so preparing for our face-to-face meeting with Jesus and our own particular judgment that we can hope to be judged fit for heaven immediately, escaping the pains of purgatory. Perhaps, if our efforts to cooperate with God's grace achieve heroic status, we will even gain a front-row seat before the Holy Trinity for eternity. Our second most important work on this planet (or any other humankind may land on in the future) is to help bring as many men and women as possible to heaven with us, through our family life, our friendships, and the sterling example we give.

See how simple it is?

Of course we know it is not that easy. But we also know that the Church provides all the instruments we need to make sure our journey through life ends in heaven: the destination that God our Father, Savior, and Sanctifier desires for us. What are these ordinary means? Principally the seven sacraments, with particular emphasis on Baptism, the Eucharist and Reconciliation, which are of necessity for salvation if available to the person; then personal prayer, with particular emphasis on meditation on Sacred Scripture (particularly the New Testament), where we learn to better know, love, and imitate Our Savior and find models of apostolic zeal in the Acts of the Apostles and the epistles of the early Church.

Of course the Church offers us much more than the basics. For example, she offers us the example of the saints throughout the ages and she safeguards our faith with the Church's teaching authority, exercised through the Pope and the bishops in communion with him. Through this authority handed down by Our Lord, faithful Christians from the earliest days of the Church have been able to stay on track, secure in Our Lord's promise that the gates of hell will not prevail against His Church. If they are faithful, they know they can await in hope Christ's second coming in glory at the Last Judgment, after which He will lead the saved to a new heaven and new earth.

And then there are the many inspirational gifts of the Catholic culture that produced Western Civilization: the chant, the hymns, cathedrals, feast days, the realist philosophy of the medieval philosophers, the sacredness of marriage and family, the music of Mozart, Beethoven, Bach, the art of Giotto, Raphael, Michelangelo, and Rubens and so many others. The list goes on and for all we know the best may lie ahead, however hard it may be to believe that from the vantage point of what sometimes looks like a cultural Dark Ages. After all, God is full of surprises for His beloved children, whom He redeemed at such a high price. Who knows what form divine inspiration will take before God shuts down the whole operation to mete out His justice and mercy according to the free choices that men and women have been making since they awoke in Eden.

None of the foregoing helps for Catholics, however, are the subject of this book. Instead, the author explores another of the great aids for Catholics, being a modern *vade mecum* (for your homework, look up that Latin phrase!) on the much neglected yet essential help to holiness known as spiritual direction. In relatively few pages, Mr. Burke has done a masterful job of explaining clearly what spiritual direction is and how you can take advantage of it.

Why is this so important now? Primarily because we are still very much at the beginning of fully applying the core message of the Second Vatican Council, i.e., the universal call to holiness. No, sanctity is not the monopoly of priests and religious, despite the great debt the Church owes to those called to those wonderful vocations. However, in the centuries ahead we are likely to see dozens, even hundreds of lay people canonized by the Church. These will be lay people who have cooperated with God's graces to grow in holiness, without (unlike most examples of lay holiness up to this point) necessarily ending their lives as martyrs.

The great majority of the saints had the help of a spiritual director of some kind on their road to holiness. Call this person a confessor, consultant, guide, or spiritual fitness trainer (my favorite), but we all need expert help us. Why? Most of all, perhaps, to avoid trusting ourselves. After all, has there ever been a saint too proud to ask advice on how to grow in holiness on his journey to eternal life? I think not—and so do you, or you would not be reading this book. I pray that you find the right person or persons to serve as spiritual guides throughout the course of your life. And now I will stop so that you can find out what you need to know from Dan Burke and then pursue this highly recommended help to holiness.

—*Rev. C. John McCloskey, Church historian and research fellow, Faith and Reason Institute in Washington (www.frmccloskey.com)*

PREFACE

In my late teens, through the grace of the Holy Spirit and the tenacity of a generous Southern Baptist pastor, I had a profound encounter with Christ that radically altered the course of my life. I came to know God in a very real, tangible, and personal way, and I learned that Christ was truly who He claimed to be. This encounter so transformed me that over the next fifteen years I spent many hours studying Scripture and the early Church fathers, eventually completing this phase of my journey by converting to Catholicism. My conversion provided the next significant leap in my life of faith as I quickly realized that I could not sit passively in the pew each Sunday and go about my life as if nothing had happened. Christ was calling me to something more. He was real; and His death, His suffering, His love, and His presence were drawing me into a deeper relationship with Him. Christ had clearly saved me from a life of darkness and despair. He had given me the gift of His body in the Eucharist and in His Church. How then could I fail to answer His call and give back to Him all that He asked of me?

I was compelled, through the prompting of the Holy Spirit and the guidance of the Church, to find my way to deeper union with Christ. But where to begin? The idea of exploring the vast depths of the Church's spiritual wealth was a great challenge; I found it daunting. Should I pursue Franciscan, Carmelite, Ignatian, or any of the many rich spiritualities and movements of the Church? What was the best way for me to grow in prayer and virtue? How could I best use the gifts and talents God had given me to serve Him and His Church?

In conversing with faithful Catholic friends, I happened across the idea of spiritual direction and was intrigued. In Protestant circles, we had mentors and mutual accountability; spiritual direction was an interesting twist on these ideas and I immediately began searching for more information. I was surprised to find very little that was helpful. While there is a lot of information available on the topic, I felt that much of it had the potential to be spiritually harmful for someone who was committed to the Church and the exclusive claims of Christ, and yet unfamiliar with Church teachings related to mystical and ascetical theology.

After searching and studying for about a year, I found my way into my first spiritual direction relationship. My relationship with this director and those since have been tremendously fruitful. Through this powerful resource, I have grown at a pace and depth in prayer and virtue that I had only experienced following my initial conversion, which was nothing less than radical. My relationship with Christ is deeper, my faith is stronger, and my sense of purpose and direction in life is firmly rooted in the reality of God's will and God's ways (by His mercy). Although my own progress is often difficult for me to see—my sins and weaknesses seem far more evident and abundant than my virtues—and while I fully recognize that I have a long way to go (my wife can attest to that!), the benefits of spiritual direction have been profound!

Yet, even with all these gains, I had had one significant, ongoing challenge: a lack of clear direction and expectations regarding the process, roles, and responsibilities of my spiritual director and me. Although I searched far and wide, I was unable to find a resource like the one you hold in your hands. From conversations with hundreds of people both within and outside of spiritual direction, I learned that many of those who desire to develop a more meaningful relationship with Christ through spiritual direction have encountered the same or similar challenges. This provided me further impetus to write this book.

Preface

Before we jump in, a little more background might be helpful regarding the approach and inspiration for this book. My entry into Catholicism has been a soul-altering adventure. Like any person of goodwill who uncovers something good, beautiful, and true, I am impassioned about sharing it with others. Empowered by His mercy and love, I am committed to giving my life to knowing Him and making Him better known to as many people as I can. Of course, in the end it is all about God's grace and the eternal sacrifice Christ made for all of us. Nevertheless, it is clear that we have the responsibility to ensure that we deliver our souls to Him in a way that's in keeping with the reality of His grace. How do we do that? We commit our lives to a relentless and joyful pursuit: the pursuit of finding the greatest and most fulfilling love relationship that any of us can experience in this life. A lived relationship with Christ brings the greatest love, joy, and peace that can be known in this life. A beautiful old Quaker hymn sums it up well:

My life flows on in endless song:
Above earth's lamentation,
I catch the sweet, tho' far-off hymn
That hails a new creation.
Through all the tumult and the strife
I hear the music ringing;
It finds an echo in my soul—
How can I keep from singing?
What tho' my joys and comfort die?
The Lord my Saviour liveth;
What tho' the darkness gather round?
Songs in the night he giveth.
No storm can shake my inmost calm,
While to that refuge clinging;
Since Christ is Lord of heaven and earth,
How can I keep from singing?

I lift my eyes; the cloud grows thin;
I see the blue above it;

And day by day this pathway smoothes,
Since first I learned to love it.
The peace of Christ makes fresh my heart,
A fountain ever springing;
All things are mine since I am his—
How can I keep from singing?

In keeping with this passion to sing of Christ through writing, several years ago I started an award-winning blog with the help of Father John Bartunek on faithful Catholic spirituality called "Roman Catholic Spiritual Direction" (www.SpiritualDirection.com). My expectation was that somewhere between seven and a hundred people might find this obscure and very narrowly focused effort helpful. To my surprise and delight, thousands responded within the first year, tens of thousands in the second, and as of this writing we have had hundreds of thousands of visitors from more than 190 countries around the world. This overwhelming response and the conversations that came about through engaging countless pilgrims seeking to deepen their relationship with Christ on the internet encouraged me to keep working on resources to nourish the souls of those who also hear the song of Christ in their hearts.

Well beyond my limited experience, this experiment has facilitated interaction with prominent Catholic writers and thinkers, spiritual directors, priests, religious, contemplative nuns, bishops, and many others who find their primary calling to be the care of souls. This near constant interaction has accelerated my learning and thinking about the spiritual life in dramatic fashion. Beyond these rich conversations, this book also draws from a wide range of resources in the hope that it will be both appealing and valuable to all seekers of God regardless of their level of experience with spiritual theology.

In my research for this book, I have also reviewed a wide range of contemporary and classic views of spiritual direction from both the Orthodox East and the Roman West and have attempted to provide a meaningful summary of a few key insights. In a straightforward and concise way, my hope is to open the spiritual treasure chest of the Church and set up a signpost that never fails to satisfy those who follow it: "All who are weary come to the waters and drink" (Is. 55:1). These are not new waters. The principles laid out here are time-tested, but without the dust on top. They have developed over the centuries and are rich with the experience of the saints and other holy souls, and with guidance and wisdom from the heart of the Church. My hope is that this simple effort will provide a light on the path to the great, but often forgotten treasures that lie waiting for any heart who sincerely desires them.

Finally, I believe that, outside of the sacraments, there is no greater or more important tool available to help us nurture our relationship with God and to grow in grace than spiritual direction. Because of this belief, I hope this book will aid you to: (1) understand spiritual direction, (2) initiate and engage in the process of spiritual direction, and (3) fully reap the spiritual benefits that Christ has waiting for you as you seek Him, find Him, and follow Him, all the days of your life.

Don't ever stop seeking and singing.

Without the unique gift and working of God in and through my wife, I would simply not have been able to write this book. To my Heavenly Father, my adoration; to her, the full extent of my earthly love and admiration; to my children, deep gratitude for their constant faithfulness to Christ and His Church.

Nobody ever writes a book without help. Some of us require far more help than others, and I am certainly one of these. The following is a list of people who have helped to encourage, inspire, unstick, and otherwise help me to complete this book. To them, and to many more, I am indebted in countless ways. For those who should have been on this list, please accept my heartfelt apology.

Becky Ward, Fr. John Bartunek, Claudia Volkman, Colin Donovan, Fr. C.J. McCloskey III, Dave Scott, Ed Constantine, Debbie Aguiar, Fr. Thomas Dubay, St. Teresa of Avila, Fr. Thomas Dailey, Sharon Lee Giganti, Michael Warsaw, and last but not least, my friends at Emmaus Road Publishing—Shannon Minch-Hughes in particular

Finally, a great note of appreciation to my family for enduring the periods in my quest when I have been less attentive than I should have been.

INTRODUCTION

Not too long ago, I came across fresh mountain lion tracks while fly-fishing alone in the Rocky Mountains of Colorado. My first response was a bit of concern, but after a brief, careful survey of the surrounding terrain, I turned my attention back to the river. As I did so, all my instincts began to press in on me and I realized that I was in a very bad situation. Facing the river and focusing on the water, I was completely unable to keep track of what was around me. The roar of the river through the canyon completely disabled my ability to hear anything but the rushing water. I tried to brush off the feeling, but the tension just continued to rise until—with a teeth-bearing growl—I decided to hike back to safety. I just couldn't get beyond the fear that the huge blind spot behind me harbored an inevitable attack.

This is a picture of a rare event in life. Blind spots are called "blind spots" because we are not aware of them; we are "blind" to them. The best among us work very hard to develop virtue and to avoid, or eliminate sin, yet often have only a vague understanding of the fragile nature of our souls. Saints and sinners alike, we all have blind spots. For all of us, the most deadly are those that threaten our spiritual health and growth. Simply put, these blind spots can hide potentially fatal attacks from the enemy of our souls. "Be sober, be watchful. Your adversary the devil prowls around like a roaring lion, seeking someone to devour. Resist him, firm in faith" (1 Pet. 5:8–9a).

However, the devil is not the only source of attack. Scripture reveals two other serious threats to our spiritual health: the world and the flesh. The world is constantly drawing us away from God. Secular culture is always raising subtle and not-so-subtle arguments against God, all the while attempting to lure us into lifestyles and choices that promise life and freedom but deliver bondage and eternal destruction: "In the world you have tribulation; but be of good cheer, I have overcome the world" (Jn. 16:33).

The last threat on our short list is "the flesh," which refers to the part of our nature that is inclined to darkness, or sin. Unfortunately, the flesh is the gateway to the soul and the door through which the world and the devil enter into the picture. Ultimately, we cannot be blindsided by the other two without the flesh providing an opening for attack: "The spirit indeed is willing, but the flesh is weak" (Mt. 26:41).

Symeon the New Theologian (AD 949 to 1022) said this: "Do not follow the wolf instead of the shepherd (cf. Mt. 7:15).... Do not be found alone, lest you be seen to be the prey of the soul-killing wolf, or as succumbing to one illness after the other, thereby dying spiritually and alone in attaining that 'woe' after you fall. For one who gives oneself to a good teacher will have no such concerns, but will live without anxiety and be saved in Christ Jesus our Lord, to whom be glory to the ages. Amen."[1]

Here Symeon reveals both the problem and the remedy. Without exception, the teachings of the saints and spiritual doctors of the Church agree: spiritual direction is among the most powerful tools to help us in the battle. Do you know any wise doctors who treat themselves when they face serious health challenges? Have you heard of any top athletes who don't have personal trainers and coaches? Spiritual direction is the means through which the Holy Spirit guides us and provides coaching for our souls. No doubt that this remedy is in itself a challenge (as most remedies are), but history books are replete with those who have chosen it and found the difficulties to be nothing when compared to the benefits.

WHAT IS SPIRITUAL DIRECTION?

Simply put, spiritual direction is a relationship through which we come to better know, love, and follow Christ through the help of a kind of spiritual coach. It is a process through which we come to know and love Christ and ultimately experience the heights of spiritual union with Him, even in this life. The director and the directee work together, through the grace and guidance of the Holy Spirit, to understand God's will, and then determine how to follow that leading in a concrete way on a day-to-day basis, into a deeper intimacy with Him. To make this idea a bit clearer, let's begin our exploration by outlining what spiritual direction is not.

Spiritual Direction Is Not a Boss/Employee Relationship

The director/directee relationship is not analogous to a boss/employee relationship. This is an area where the language of spiritual direction can be a bit confusing in our culture. In normal usage, a "director" tells the one who is directed what to do. Implied is an authority that has punitive power—the power to punish or withhold rewards in the case of disobedience. This is not at all the case with healthy spiritual direction. The directee in this case would be better compared to an athlete and the director a personal coach—specifically, a spiritual fitness coach. Just as with a coach in any sport, the athlete is the one that is ultimately in control. He or she hires a personal coach to help them achieve otherwise elusive goals and perspectives. In the end, the level of influence the

3

director has over the directee is based on the directee's free choice rather than any position of power. Another helpful comparison common in the East is that of a spiritual healer or physician. Either way, the directee always has the free choice to seek out and follow—or not follow—the healing and growth available to them through the spiritual director as they seek together to understand and cooperate with God's work.

Spiritual Direction Is Not Confession

Spiritual direction is not synonymous with confession. The challenge with distinguishing spiritual direction from confession usually comes when the modern inquirer reads the saints who talk about their spiritual director or confessor as if they are one and the same thing. The reason for this is that there was a time when it was very common for confession and spiritual direction to take place together. The modern decline in priest-to-parishioner ratio has likely been the unfortunate cause of the separation of the two activities, but spiritual direction has never been the exclusive territory of priests or even religious. As an example, most would be surprised to know that Pope John Paul II, in his youth, had a lay spiritual director. Regardless, even though this is a sub-optimal situation, at present, confession and spiritual direction are more likely to occur as two separate activities.

Spiritual Direction Is Not Spiritual Friendship

Spiritual friendships are invaluable to the life of a Christian, and while they share many characteristics with spiritual direction, they differ in a few very important ways. One key difference is that the specific focus of spiritual direction is the spiritual life of the directee. Spiritual friendships and mentoring relationships frequently include aspects of the spiritual life, yet they usually also have elements, activities, and interests that are peripheral (though sometimes beneficial) to the spiritual life. Another key difference is with respect to the intensity of the relationship; going back to the personal coach analogy, most athletes would never expect to have a friendly or passive level of accountability with a personal coach. Instead, they engage with a personal coach to be firmly challenged, pushed, and encouraged toward concrete progress. Again, the directee is ultimately in control, but when he or she seeks out a director, they are typically looking for a much higher level of accountability and direction than the normal bounds of friendships can often provide—even healthy spiritual friendships.

Spiritual Direction Is Not a Catholic Self-Help Program

Self-sufficiency, self-reliance, and even self-centeredness are promoted in our culture, but are damaging to souls when they bleed into the spiritual life. As the Introduction illustrates, when we have a blind spot we cannot rely solely on our own limited capacity to see what we do not perceive—no matter how hard we might try. Instead, we need to break the pattern of a false, bootstrap spirituality that often results in self-delusion and spiritual atrophy. As St. Bernard once said, "He who constitutes himself his own director becomes the disciple of a fool."[2] In keeping with this challenging insight, we misunderstand spiritual direction if we think we just need a quick pep talk to get back on our feet and get going on our own again. Still, even though logically compelling, the idea of moving beyond self-help is a tough pill for most of us to swallow.

Spiritual Direction Is Not Psychological Counseling

The psychological and physical aspects of our lives have an impact on our spiritual lives, and there is no easy way to extricate these realities from one another. Your spiritual life can and will affect you emotionally. If these emotions prove to be a hindrance to your spiritual progress, they should be addressed with your spiritual director. Conversely, your spiritual life, as it grows, will positively impact your psychological and physical health. Yet, just as you would not go to a spiritual director for physical therapy, it is also unwise to attempt to deal with deep psychological issues with a spiritual director (at least with one who has not received special training in both fields). When emotional or psychological issues are serious, seek specially trained professionals for help.

Spiritual Direction Is Not a Onetime Emergency-Room Event

Under normal circumstances, spiritual direction should not be thought of as being comparable to an emergency room visit. Spiritual direction is better likened to a wellness program or a long-term exercise and diet commitment that will result in maximum health. Even though there is a place for appropriate emergency calls to one's spiritual director, these typically occur within the context of ongoing spiritual direction. In general, it is not reasonable to expect a spiritual director to be responsive to emergent needs outside of an ongoing relationship. Why? Because experienced spiritual directors understand that if a person experiencing an emergency is not ready to work diligently and consistently on their relationship with God (both at the point of crisis and afterward), the director is likely unable to assist in any substantive way. That said, some individuals in crisis experience a level of clarity that could be the beginning of a serious and life-altering faith commitment. Those in this category are ready and eager to do whatever is necessary to pursue God and cooperate with His work in their soul. These are not in the same camp as those who have a heart attack, receive emergency services, and then return to the lifestyle that brought them to their knees in the first place. The good news is that God is always ready to receive us when we are ready to turn to Him.

Spiritual Direction Is Not Wandering Around with a Spiritual Companion

Wandering around is the opposite of a deliberate journey in a specific direction. Spiritual direction that is directionless is a contradiction. Some modern conceptions of spiritual direction have reduced the director-directee relationship to one of blind companions in spiritual meandering and self-discovery. This is not a picture of healthy spiritual direction. Spiritual direction that lacks direction is not direction at all. It may make both parties feel good about one another, but if the desired end is not union with Christ, and if a specific path does not emerge for the directee to follow in order to better know and love Christ and others, then the relationship cannot rightly be called spiritual direction.

Spiritual Direction Is Not a "Just Me and Jesus" or a "Just Me and the Holy Spirit" Effort

Those that struggle with self-disclosure or a lack of understanding of the definition and benefits of spiritual direction sometimes end up rationalizing their weakness by discounting the need for human assistance. "Just me and Jesus" or "Just me and the Holy Spirit" becomes their slogan. This is a comfortable but dangerous trap. As we will discuss later, God has chosen to use human instruments to shape, mold, and bring us closer to Him. This is because it can be very dangerous to direct oneself; the devil lurks in that blind spot and waits to attack; others can see our faults and weaknesses better than we can, and a good director can tell us what's hiding in our blind spot. It is extremely rare that anyone seeking to deepen their faith will find themselves in circumstances where God violates His chosen means for our growth. Unless you are a desert hermit, you are not likely to fall into this category (and even hermits have spiritual directors).

Spiritual Direction Is Not about Apostolic Work

Though this problem may be limited to a few modern movements, it is worth noting. If a priest, consecrated, or religious is engaged with a person in apostolic work and is also serving as that individual's spiritual director, the work of the apostolate can easily displace authentic spiritual direction. Spiritual direction should include the pursuit of virtue and action in faith, but the emphasis must always be first on a relationship with Christ, and then only secondarily on the ways in which that relationship plays out in specific apostolic action. Leave the nuts and bolts of Kingdom work for meetings specifically on that topic. This way, both of these activities will be treated with the appropriate emphasis.

Spiritual Direction Is Not Just About Prayer— and It's Not Just About Action

Though this form of direction doesn't belong fully in the "this is not spiritual direction" category, it can reflect an immature form of direction not likely to yield the growth that comes from a more balanced approach. Love for God in the form of prayer or adoration could very well be a false love if it does not result in tangible expressions of love for those around us. The converse is also true: if we give our lives to social justice but ignore the source of justice, we are like Martha, in danger of missing "the better part" and failing to fulfill both of the commandments that Jesus affirmed as the greatest (see Mt. 22:38).

Spiritual Direction Is...

Now that we are clear on what spiritual direction is not, we can focus on what spiritual direction is.

Spiritual direction is a relationship between three persons:

- the Holy Spirit
- the director
- the directee

The main focus of spiritual direction is union with God. The central aim of spiritual direction is to help guide the directee to purposefully, consistently, and substantively grow in their relationship with God and neighbor.

This will happen by discovering God's presence and work in our souls and embracing His will through the fruitful embrace of prayer and virtue. The ultimate end of spiritual direction is, as Jesus commanded, to "love the Lord your God with all your heart, and with all your soul, and with all your mind, and with all your strength" and to "love your neighbor as yourself" (Mk. 12:30–31). Spiritual direction is about developing a love relationship with God that inevitably spills into all other areas of our lives.

With this concise overview of spiritual direction, in the next chapter we'll explore whether or not spiritual direction is right for you.

Spiritual Guides, Spiritual Directors, and Spiritual Mentors: What's the Difference?

Depending upon the source of the spiritual director's training, there are different types or titles of those who offer spiritual direction. For instance, a number of movements in the Church offer training for laypeople so that they can provide spiritual direction. These organizations often make a distinction between ordained (men) or consecrated (men or women), referring to them as "spiritual directors," and laypersons who might be called "spiritual guides" or "spiritual mentors." The distinction is usually a reflection of the level of training and education possessed by the one providing the guidance. It is likely that those with the title "spiritual director" have received a level of formation that is higher than those who might be called "spiritual mentors" or "spiritual guides."

Avoid getting caught up in the specific titles. Nor should you assume that someone with a lower level of formation is insufficiently equipped to help you with your spiritual life. Spending time with another soul that is aggressively pursuing Christ, and has some experience that exceeds yours can be very beneficial. The goal is to understand and pursue Christ in the process regardless of the specific titles that may or may not be applied to the individuals available to help you do so.

DO I REALLY NEED SPIRITUAL DIRECTION?

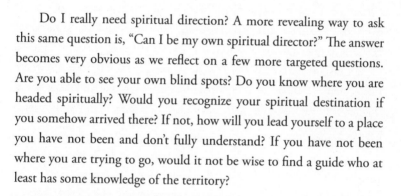

Do I really need spiritual direction? A more revealing way to ask this same question is, "Can I be my own spiritual director?" The answer becomes very obvious as we reflect on a few more targeted questions. Are you able to see your own blind spots? Do you know where you are headed spiritually? Would you recognize your spiritual destination if you somehow arrived there? If not, how will you lead yourself to a place you have not been and don't fully understand? If you have not been where you are trying to go, would it not be wise to find a guide who at least has some knowledge of the territory?

Without a guide we run the risk of losing our way or venturing down paths that can waste precious time as we seek our eternal destination. As St. Jerome once noted, "Do not be your own master and do not set out upon a way that is entirely new for you without a guide; otherwise you will soon go astray." Similarly, St. Augustine said, "As a blind man cannot follow the good road without a leader, no one can walk without a guide." St. Vincent Ferrer strongly asserts, "Our Lord Jesus Christ, without whom we can do nothing, will not give his grace to him who, though he has access to an expert guide, rejects this precious means of sanctification, thinking that he can look after on his own everything that touches on his salvation. He who has a director...will reach his goal more easily and more quickly than if he acted as his own guide, even if he be very intelligent and have the very best of spiritual books."[3]

Moving beyond the untenable notion that we can be our own spiritual director (or the "me and the Holy Spirit" approach we discussed earlier), we should also reflect on the fact that God works through people. In all of human history, the Incarnation is the most spectacular illustration of this. God was determined to restore us to relationship with Him. Did He stay far off and toss down a few books and yell, "Figure it out on your own!"? Instead, knowing the fallen human heart, He determined that it was better to become one of us, and chose to manifest Himself through the most human of relationships, through the consent of a human being, our Blessed Mother. In this way, the Holy Spirit overshadowed her, conceived His son in her womb, and Jesus submitted Himself to rest in her protection until He was born in the most humble of circumstances. In this humility, He chose to reveal His love and desire for us, and He allows us to attain some understanding and response to that love through the uniquely human and tangible reality of interpersonal relationships.

After His resurrection, as He left this earth and ascended into heaven, He provided the Holy Spirit and the Church to further our restoration, healing, and sanctification. How do the Holy Spirit and the Church work? In and through people! A cursory review of the New Testament makes this overwhelmingly obvious. You won't find even a hint of the idea of a lone-wolf Christian who is not dependent upon others for their spiritual needs (or physical for that matter). What you will find is God working in and amongst His people as they rely upon and serve one another toward Him. Just one example is the striking conversion of St. Paul in the ninth chapter of the book of Acts. On the way to Damascus he had a profound encounter with Christ that was to completely change the direction of his life. Even with that powerful personal encounter, St. Paul did not then have all that he needed to understand the next steps he should take. Instead, Jesus directed Paul to a person, Ananias, to whom God revealed what Paul should do. Why did God work this way? It is a mystery, but it is clear that in His providence and provision He works through people to help us to Him. In *The Dialogue* (7), St. Catherine of Siena reveals this perspective on the work of God through dependence on others (from God the Father):

> The same is true of many of my gifts and graces, virtues and other spiritual gifts, and those things necessary for the body and human life. I have distributed them all in such a way that no one has all of them. Thus I have given you reason—necessity, in fact—to practice mutual charity. For I could well have supplied you with all your needs, both spiritual and material. But I wanted to make you dependent on one another." St. John of the Cross echoed this idea when he boldly stated, "God so desires that man place himself under the direction of another, that He absolutely does not want to see us give full assent to the supernatural truths He Himself imparts, before they have issued out of the mouth of a man.[4]

Pope John Paul II wrote in *Christifidelis Laici* (58), "To be able to discover the actual will of the Lord in our lives always involves the following: a receptive listening to the Word of God and the Church, fervent and constant prayer, recourse to a wise and loving spiritual guide, and a faithful discernment of the gifts and talents given by God...."[5] On the same topic the *Catechism of the Catholic Church* (2695) notes that "Ordained ministers, the consecrated life, catechesis, prayer groups, and 'spiritual direction' ensure assistance within the Church in the practice of prayer." Finally, even a cursory review of the writings of doctors of the Church reveal references to spiritual direction that are too numerous to catalogue. The bottom line is that spiritual direction is a gift that the serious spiritual pilgrim cannot do without.

HOW DO I KNOW IF I AM READY FOR SPIRITUAL DIRECTION?

How do I know if I am ready for spiritual direction? This question is worth exploring, because without the answer you may wander into a spiritual direction relationship and walk away even more disappointed and frustrated than when you began.

One common indication that you are ready for spiritual direction is that you are tired of stumbling around on your own in the sometimes-darkness of the spiritual life. You have discovered by your own experience one of the secrets of the saints: We absolutely cannot make it on our own. Bootstrap self-help Christianity bears no resemblance to God's plan for us and is directly contrary to His revealed design of engagement with us. As well, after the Fall we have another enemy to contend with, an internal tendency toward self-deception and sin. Yes, we bear the image of God and, bearers of that image, we are essentially good, but we also see ourselves and God through the distorted lens of our sin, the sins of our forefathers, and the deception of the world. Without some external help to clean the windshield, we are headed for a crash.

Many committed Catholics find themselves in a position where they know they are not growing as they should, and they recognize the lack of fruit in their lives that reflects the obvious work and presence of Christ. They recognize they are in the right place (i.e., the Catholic Church) but feel empty, unfulfilled, or even just off-track. Often they find themselves suffering from their own life decisions and not knowing how to break out of patterns of sin and despair. Sometimes it is just a nagging lack of peace that says, "There has got to be more to this life."

Another indicator of readiness surfaces with those who do not come from a life of habitual sin but simply from quiet mediocrity. They may regularly participate in the sacraments, they may not suffer from habitual mortal or even patterns of venial sin, but still, they long for something more. They may just experience a vague draw to go deeper in prayer, to engage more fully with Christ. This sometimes subtle draw to find something more in their faith and relationship with God is a clear sign of God's ever-present invitation to go deeper.

The final characteristic is that you may have some sense that further progress in your inner life cannot be made without a purposeful infusion of energy. You recognize that only a fool stands out in front of an exercise facility and then upon entry lays down to take a nap. Spiritual direction, because it deals with the deepest and most substantive issues of life, is never easy; the believer is now entering into territory that the enemy of souls fears most and will oppose with great force and frequency. Those who enter into the serious spiritual life without a strong commitment to persevere will likely self-eject from the process and find themselves in a worse state than when they began. In this latter case, the enemy is then firmly in control of defeated territory and the one who is defeated knows he has lost—a much worse state than the false peace of blissful ignorance. The answer? The seeker must make a life-time commitment to fight their way to God. They must commit to rising every time they fall, taking full responsibility for their spiritual life and growth, and never letting go of the idea that God is always ready to receive and strengthen us when we turn to Him; even when our falls are severe.

Regardless of which of these camps one emerges from, all come with some measure of wisdom and humility (even if very slight), and a recognition that they cannot travel the path to God without assistance.

This leads them to a readiness (even if reluctant) to reveal the inner workings of their soul to another and ask for help. This recognition of the need for a guide, coupled with sufficient tenacity to deal with the requirements of honesty and vulnerability, is the beginning of a new journey deeper into Christ. If any of these factors describe you in any way, be assured, you are ready.

How many people do you know who could benefit from reading this book?

Visit **DynamicCatholic.com** and request SIX copies for just $18.

HOW DO I KNOW IF I AM NOT READY FOR SPIRITUAL DIRECTION?

How do I know if I am *not* ready for spiritual direction? The key here is to follow God's lead. If the characteristics of readiness above are present in you, it is safe to assume that you are feeling the call of God into a deeper relationship. Don't hesitate, but aggressively follow that call. That said, there are also certain hindrances that can and should be dealt with before meeting with a spiritual director.

Father Reginald Garragou-LaGrange makes the relevant observation that "pride is a bandage over the eyes of our spirit, which hinders us from seeking the truth, especially that relative to the majesty of God and the excellence of those who surpass us. It prevents us from wishing to be instructed by them, or it prompts us not to accept direction without argument."[6] In this thought he reveals the single greatest hindrance to progress in spiritual direction: pride. This stifling sin manifests itself in many ways. The most difficult to deal with is when the seeker already exhibits some measure of holiness and spiritual discipline. For instance, many saints and spiritual writers have struggled with the reasons why daily Mass attendees often have behaviors, attitudes, or life patterns that are very contrary to what would be expected of someone who encounters Christ every day in the Eucharist. I agree with those who have concluded that the reason is a lack of mental prayer and of the exercise of very specific efforts to develop and live virtues on a daily basis. So, the daily communicant or the person who prays the Rosary every day might point to the great depth of their commitment and argue against any suggestion that there is more that is necessary for their spiritual growth or salvation. This can then result in a self-protecting pride that does not allow for recognition of other faults. In effect, any spiritual practice pursued for the wrong reasons will produce or reinforce blind spots that are then even more severe because they are solidified in pride, shallow or merely human virtue, and self-justification.

Those who suffer with these issues are often very picky (for the wrong reasons) about who they might choose for a spiritual director. The committed Catholic or seasoned Christian warrior may be seeking the wise old priest-sage who prays four hours a day and has the gift of seeing souls, when they may need a holy layperson who may not have a doctorate in dogmatic theology, but who clearly understands the path of humility and what it means to have a vibrant relationship with Christ.

The next challenge is similar to the one above and has its root in the sin of vanity. Because we naturally want people we revere to think highly of us, we often seek to manage their perceptions of us. Don't worry; if you find yourself here you are in good company. St. Teresa of Avila alludes to this struggle even among holy people. The key issue here is the readiness to fight the battle of being open and transparent. You wouldn't take serious health challenges to a doctor and then hide symptoms, would you? Admittedly, physical challenges are much easier to discuss than those things that we might worry would cast a bad light on our character. Yet, the spiritual journey is far more consequential than our physical one. When we seek out a spiritual director, we need to work diligently to bare our souls as openly and honestly as we can. Otherwise, our directors, not knowing the truth, will be unable to make an accurate assessment and it's unlikely that we will make progress. As St. Francis de Sales wisely encourages:

> Go to your confessor, open your heart thoroughly, let him see every corner of your soul, and take all his advice with the utmost simplicity and humility, for God loves obedience, and He often

makes the counsel we take, especially that of the guides of souls, to be more useful than would seem likely; just as He caused the waters of the Jordan, commended by Elijah to Naaman, to cure his leprosy in spite of the improbability to human reason.[7]

Another hindrance to a healthy entry into spiritual direction falls into the area of spiritual sloth. The expectation is that the director will now lead me in my spiritual life. We discussed this error in our initial analogy of spiritual direction being similar to the efforts of a personal trainer. In this relationship, the trainer does not take the lead. They do not approach the athlete; they do not establish the level of motivation within the athlete. They merely facilitate the growth that the athlete is already seeking, already owns, already desires, and is already committed to. This may seem like an unimportant point but it is a common error: expecting a spiritual director to set the course of our spiritual life and then, in any way, to maintain that course on our behalf.

If the seeker recognizes these weaknesses as true to their condition, it is still likely that they are called to a spiritual direction relationship. No matter what the circumstance, we are all called to move deeper in our union with Christ until the day we see Him face-to-face. If the seeker also experiences the positive characteristics listed in the previous section, they should move forward to engage in spiritual direction. They should, however, exercise ownership, great diligence, and openness with their directors to prevent the effort from becoming an empty exercise of false piety that only further endangers the soul.

HOW DO I FIND AND SELECT
A SPIRITUAL DIRECTOR?

Good spiritual directors can be found among priests, religious, and lay members of the Church, and there are benefits and drawbacks to each depending on the situation. For instance, there are some religious orders that receive extensive formation, or specific training, and are well prepared to provide spiritual direction; others are not. It is not common for diocesan priests to have received formation specifically for the purposes of providing spiritual direction. With all priests or religious, however, if the formation they have received is faithful to the magisterium, they should have a reasonable foundation in dogmatic or moral theology, which provides a sound base of knowledge and understanding to navigate the spiritual life. This is particularly true if they are actively pursuing their own spiritual growth.

With respect to lay spiritual directors, some might be surprised to know that early in his spiritual journey, Blessed Pope John Paul II received direction from a layperson. As well, the first Christians who were broadly known for their spiritual direction were the hermits of the Eastern Churches—who were laymen. That said, it is ideal to have a well-trained spiritual director that is also your confessor. There are no guarantees; yet we should remember that God does, and will, provide for our needs. Spiritual depth will emerge with effort, and it is up to the seeker to search out and find the soul that God has waiting for them.

Within this broad range of options (laypersons, priests, religious, etc.), universally accepted norms for training or certification of spiritual directors do not exist. Some of the governing or certifying bodies for spiritual directors and schools for spiritual directors are far from faithful to authentic Catholic spirituality. That said, three faithful schools in the U.S. that provide sound training for spiritual directors are listed in the appendix. Even with the emergence of these faithful and much-needed efforts, it is distressing that the seeker is just as likely to find harmful New Age or non-Catholic spirituality disguised as Catholic teaching as they are to find the real thing. But don't be discouraged. There is a clear way through these challenges and even a potential shortcut that we will discuss later. In the meantime, let's consider how a serious Catholic can navigate these hazardous waters and find the assistance they need to grow in their faith.

Preparing for the Search

As part of any spiritual growth program, the seeker must be prepared to focus energies toward the preeminent goal of dynamic union with Christ. One critical aspect of this journey involves intellectual formation through spiritual reading and study, leading to a more mature ability to discern truth from error. A life-habit of regular spiritual reading and study is a key to successful navigation around the dangers of human frailty and deception (including self-deception). Regular reading and study prepare and arm us for the "spiritual warfare" we will encounter as we get serious about our spiritual life.

When training people to detect counterfeit money, the secret is familiarity with the real thing, not with the thousands of approaches to counterfeit bills. In the same way, if we develop our understanding of the one true Faith, we are far less likely to accept a counterfeit. With respect to spiritual directors, and retreat centers for that matter, a common area of counterfeit spirituality is the confusion (sometimes well intended) between Catholic forms of spirituality and those of other faith traditions. To avoid these distractions the directee must acquire an understanding of prayer from two foundational angles. First, they should become familiar with the *Catechism of the Catholic Church* on the topic of prayer (Part IV). It is not only helpful with respect to definitions but is also concise, beautiful, inspiring, and completely trustworthy in its treatment of prayer. Second, there are two recent documents provided by the Church that review points of discernment regarding the distinctions between faithful Catholic tradition and common forms of confusion found in the Church today:

Jesus Christ, The Bearer of the Water of Life: A Christian Reflection on the "New Age." Produced by the Pontifical Council for Culture and the Pontifical Council for Interreligious Dialogue, this document evaluates many aspects of "New Age" spirituality from an authentically Christian perspective. It is especially helpful in demonstrating how it is that many of the New Age movement's core concepts and practices not only differ from but often contradict the Christian faith. We're told in the opening chapter (p. 9): "This document guides those involved in pastoral work in their understanding and response to New Age spirituality, both illustrating the points where this spirituality contrasts with the Catholic faith and refuting the positions espoused by New Age thinkers in opposition to Christian faith." This document can be found through a search on the Vatican web site at www.vatican.va.[8]

Letter to the Bishops of the Catholic Church on Some Aspects of Christian Meditation. This document was prepared by then Cardinal Ratzinger (now Pope Benedict XVI) to deal with widespread confusion regarding some of what is called Centering Prayer and other well-intended but misguided attempts to blend Christian and non-Christian forms of prayer. Because this document is so important and addresses the most common challenges in teachings on prayer that a directee might find in spiritual direction or at a retreat center, we have provided the complete text in Appendix Two of this book. It is well worth reading several times in order to absorb the reflections of Cardinal Ratzinger on authentic Christian prayer.

Faithful Guidance in the Spiritual Life

If you have not yet started a program of reading to develop your spiritual life, another great place to begin is with the doctors of the Church. "Doctor" of the Church is a special title accorded by the Church to certain saints, which indicates that their teachings are exceptionally useful to Christians in any age. These men and women are particularly known both for their timeless depth of understanding and the orthodoxy of their teachings. At present there are thirty-five doctors of the Church. A subset of these doctors wrote extensively on the topics of prayer and the spiritual life. Among them are St. Teresa of Avila, St. John of the Cross, St. Francis de Sales, St. Bernard of Clairvaux, St. Catherine of Sienna, and St. Thérèse of Lisieux.

One point of caution is in order here. It is common for popular authors and speakers who teach about prayer and the spiritual life to quote from these saints. Merely quoting a saint does not ensure fidelity to their intent. The works of these saints should be read and understood firsthand, along with solid guides to their works. Modern authors like Dr. Ralph Martin, Fr. Timothy Gallagher, Fr. Thomas Dubay, Fr. Jacques Philippe, Fr. John Bartunek, and Fr. Benedict Groeschel are examples of trustworthy sources of the rich beauty and depth of authentic Catholic spirituality. As a general rule, there are publishers who are specifically dedicated to producing faithful Catholic materials. Emmaus Road and Ignatius Press are both great examples. It is not likely that you will find a book in their catalogues that contradict or distort the teachings of the Church.

If you want your reading to be on unshakeable ground, begin your program of self-education with the *Catechism*. Simply set a goal of reading daily for five to ten minutes (or even every Saturday or Sunday for a longer period). You will be surprised how far you can get with a small but consistent investment of time. Once you complete your reading of the *Catechism* (at least on the subject of prayer), I strongly recommend reading Fr. Thomas Dubay's *Prayer Primer: Igniting a Fire Within* (Ignatius Press) to gain a solid foundation about Church teaching and tradition on each of the different forms of prayer mentioned in the *Catechism*. Even if you find the readings dry (though most don't), don't let that distract you from gaining the knowledge you need to ensure you are not led astray by potentially harmful or confusing spiritual detours.

If the above suggestions feel a bit intimidating, don't worry. You may want to start your program of spiritual reading with some other titles that present the richness of the Catholic world view with less emphasis on methods of prayer. Fr. Eugene Boylan's *This Tremendous Lover*, Frank Sheed's *Theology for Beginners* and *Theology and Sanity*, and even St. Francis de Sales *Introduction to the Devout Life* were all written for lay Catholics who recognize the call to move ever deeper into their relationship with God.

Finding a Needle in a Haystack

With this initial reading program under way, you can begin to identify possible directors in your area. It would be misleading to even hint that finding good spiritual direction is easy. Still, be assured that as you seek with an open and relentless heart, God will lead you to the right place at the right time, even if that place is simply working through the frustration involved with finding good direction. There are a number of helpful places you can look; here's a short list of possibilities:

Call your diocesan office for leads. There are several types of leads you can find by calling your diocese. First, they can point you to those known for spiritual direction in your area. Second, they can also provide you with a list of local religious orders or retreat centers. Don't hesitate to venture beyond your own diocesan boundaries if the list of options runs too short. This might be particularly necessary if you don't live in a major metropolitan area.

Take a second look in the local confessionals. If you have found a good confessor, a priest who has been particularly helpful to you with advice or dialogue during or after confession, don't hesitate to ask him one simple question to determine if he might be able to provide you with direction: "I would be grateful if I can follow up with you on this matter in the near future; can I call you for an appointment?" We will cover this approach later in more detail.

Consider your parish priest. Often, excessive concern about what others might think can keep us from reaching out to those who are close to us. Don't fall into this trap. Good directors are hard to find. If your parish priest is a good candidate, don't miss the opportunity. Another common worry in this area is the workload of a particular priest. However, this is really for the priest to decide, not the potential directee. As we will cover later, if you are an eager and attentive pilgrim, many parish priests will figure out how to make it work.

Connect with faithful Catholic affiliation groups in your parish or diocese. If you have faithful groups or parish programs in your diocese like Catholics United for the Faith, ENDOW,[9] Walking with Purpose,[10] Catholic Scripture Studies,[11] Disciples of Jesus and Mary,[12] or others, begin attending their meetings and connecting with people who take their faith seriously. Then ask around; often the best leads come from personal recommendations.

Seek support through personal relationships. When you engage in your local parish or activities that include faithful formation, you will likely recognize the same people showing up for these events on a regular basis. Get to know them. They are probably living at a level of deeper engagement with their faith, and some may have spiritual directors or can point you to solid confessors that may be good candidates to assist you.

Keep in mind that this could be a long process, and if you are called to it you need to maintain your commitment for as long as it takes. God knows your needs: He desires to bring you closer to Himself and He will do so as long as you keep striving and stumbling towards Him. Sometimes the painstaking search for a director is just as important as the process of spiritual direction itself.

Finding the Real Thing

A few final thoughts about selecting a spiritual director (before we get to the shortcut). The importance of magisterial faithfulness might be illusive to some. After all, if the person holding themselves up to be a spiritual director is committed enough to be a priest, nun, or whatever, and they say they love Jesus, what's the big deal? Well, if, like me, you have had major surgery, wouldn't you want someone who is a specialist in your specific area of need to operate on you? Would you entrust yourself to a dentist who confidently informed you that he could also remove your gallbladder? Now, I have seen dentists whose medical garb is similar to that of the doctor who removed my gallbladder; but they are committed to completely different disciplines with completely different skills and education. We have also seen doctors in the news who claim the Hippocratic Oath but who instead prove dangerous to the lives of children and the elderly.

With the spiritual life, we are looking to tap into the pure source of real life, Christ Himself. He established a real, living, physical expression of His love and guidance, the Church. The Church has provided sound and unwavering teaching on doctrine and morals for thousands of years, even in the midst of the corruption of too many of its members. She is the only sure and complete source of trustworthy guidance to her Holy King. Only those who are in authentic submission to Christ's chosen means of salvation can help us to acquire that same gift. Those who claim to love Christ and His way but who accept some and reject others of His teachings in a manner similar to those shopping for shoes, are themselves lost and are not fit to lead anyone else to the fullness of faith.

With this understanding, it can be a challenge to determine where the potential spiritual director stands on matters that are not peripheral in the eyes of the Church. There are a few hot-button issues that you can probe to determine the level of commitment any potential director has with respect to Church teaching. The first is abortion. If the prospective director is not unhesitatingly opposed to this intrinsic evil, then you are talking to the wrong person. If, when asked, they begin their response with, "Well, abortion is one of many life issues," there is a strong possibility that they are not a trustworthy guide in matters of faith and morals. This kind of response is often merely a ruse for a wayward perspective.

Another of these issues is an encyclical penned by Pope Paul VI entitled *Humanae Vitae*. If you don't get a positive response when you ask about this document, look elsewhere (oh, and you might want to read it yourself!). A third issue is regarding the authority of the Church and our duty as faithful Catholics to honor that authority. To better understand the magisterial authority of the Church, you will find *Mysterium Ecclesiae* (In Defense of the Catholic Doctrine on the Church) to be helpful. You can find these documents on the Vatican website, www.vatican.va. If you take the time to review these brief but profound documents, you will find yourself armed with the means to interpret clear indicators of the magisterial commitment of any director. You also might find yourself in the challenging position of changing your own views on the central matters of our faith—a great subject for spiritual direction! Feel free to ask your potential director what they think about the subjects covered in these documents. If you get anything but immediate affirmation, be cautious and respectfully ask more questions. By doing this you are not being arrogant or judgmental. On the contrary, you are being humble and wise! As Catholics we are privileged to be able to know clearly when our leaders are on the wrong track—that's one reason why the Church gives us a universal Catechism.

It's one thing to talk about faith and spirituality, quite another to live i; an effective spiritual director must have experience in the spiritual life.

St. John of the Cross, in his comments on stanza three of "The Living Flame of Love," strongly states that unless a director has some experience in the spiritual life he or she cannot be of benefit to the directee and will likely do harm. If we are to follow the lead of someone in our spiritual lives, they must have at least some experience in the life they are leading us into.

What we are seeking in spiritual direction is not fully realized in mere factual information. We are seeking to more deeply engage with the person of Christ Himself. We are pursuing a relationship of love, not an academic exercise. Those whom we choose to lead us must already know this great love—not just know about it—if they are to effectively lead us to it.

Questions for Your Would-Be Spiritual Director

Within the context of these key issues, here is a brief list of suggested questions you might ask a prospective spiritual director to determine if they are a fit for you:

- Are you in regular spiritual direction? How often do you meet with your director?

- What has motivated you to become a spiritual director?

- Can you tell me a little about your spiritual disciplines and spiritual life (Mass, Adoration, meditation, Rosary, mental prayer, etc.)?

- Do you have any theological or spiritual formation or other special training to help you as a spiritual director?

- How long have you been a spiritual director?

- Are there any teachings of the Church that you disagree with or struggle with?

- Do you have a devotion to Mary?

- Please tell me about your relationship with Christ.

If you feel uncomfortable asking these questions face-to-face, then try using email. You can soften your inquiry by saying something like, "I am looking for a particular approach in spiritual direction. Would you mind if I asked you a few questions about your perspective?" They will of course answer with something like, "Yes, feel free." You can then say "thank you" and provide your list of questions to them. Asking these questions might be uncomfortable, but it is far better to do this up front than to find yourself unraveling a relationship with a director who is providing direction to a destination that is different than the one you are seeking.

A Potential Shortcut

There is no healthy way around the need for directees to have a solid understanding of their faith. However, semi-shortcuts through this maze can be found in the many faithful movements and orders within the Church. Those that have maintained a solid grip on authentic Catholicism often provide means for their members to deepen their faith in many helpful ways, including spiritual direction. Essentially, when approaching these organizations we are looking to adopt a rule of life. That is, we are looking for a specific spiritual path that can help to focus our spiritual disciplines and practice of virtue.

Often these organizations follow the fruitful paths of the saints who founded them (like St. Francis and the Franciscans), or those who played significant roles within them (like St. John of the Cross or St. Teresa of Avila in the Carmelite tradition). Obviously, becoming a third-order or lay Carmelite or Franciscan is a serious commitment. For those who take their faith seriously, these commitments have benefits that far outweigh any related challenges.

To be clear, it is not necessary to become a cloistered nun or a hermit to reap the benefits of these beautiful gifts to the Church. Lay organizations are available for people just like you and me. A few good examples of more recent spiritualities that have been approved by the

Church are Opus Dei (www.opusdei.org), Apostles of the Interior Life (www.apostolevitainteriore.it), Communion and Liberation (www.clonline.org), and Regnum Christi (www.regnumchristi.com). As well, Secular Institutes can provide a great deal of support for their member's spiritual and apostolic living. You can find more information at www.secularinstitutes.org. The constitutions or canonical provisions of these and many more are approved by the Holy See, and the direction they provide for the spiritual life can be of enormous spiritual value. You can contact these organizations via their websites to find information about activities in your area.

A good resource to determine the faithfulness of any group like this can be found in Catholic Culture's reviews of the websites of various organizations (www.catholicculture.org/culture/reviews). If Catholic Culture deems the content of their website questionable, this doesn't mean that you won't find faithful members who might be able to assist you, but be cautious and aware. If you find, for instance, that you are drawn to Carmelite spirituality, do a little research and contact the representatives closest to you. But always take care to ask those questions you would ask of any potential spiritual director. If any red flags surface, never hesitate to gently and respectfully inquire about the details. After all, you are entrusting your soul into someone's care, and only a fool would do that without serious inquiry.

To wrap up this section we return to St. Symeon the New Theologian, who provides us with some profound advice on selecting a spiritual director:

> Seek out one who is, if you will, an intercessor, a physician, and a good counselor; a good counselor, that he may offer ways of repentance which agree with his good advice; a physician, that he may prescribe the appropriate medicine for each of your wounds; and an intercessor, that he may propitiate God, standing before Him face to face, and offering Him prayer and

intercession on your behalf. Do not try to find some flatterer or slave to his belly and make him your counselor and ally lest, by accommodating himself to your will and not to what God desires, he teach you what you would like to hear and leave you in reality an unreconciled enemy. Nor should you choose an inexperienced physician lest, by his over-aggressiveness and untimely incisions and cauterizations, he plunge you into the depth of despair or, worse, allow you by his extreme sympathy to think you are getting better when in fact you are still unwell, and so deliver you to the eternal hell which you had not expected. For this does no more than cause in us the very illness that is already killing the soul.[13]

HOW DO I SET UP AND PREPARE FOR MY FIRST MEETING?

Often, the most difficult aspect of setting the first meeting is apprehension. All those who desire a spiritual director and do not yet have one are in the same vulnerable position. The following is an overview of common struggles that you might encounter. Sometimes just knowing that you are not alone can be a help in gaining the courage necessary to overcome these challenges. After we cover these common challenges, we will review how to go about the basic preparation and setup for your meeting. We will also provide guidance on key aspects of the approach necessary for effective direction.

Common Challenges and Perspective

- The area of our lives that is most important to us (our faith) is at a place where we obviously need help in order to grow. This can be a difficult and sensitive admission, especially for men.

- Committed Catholics typically hold priests and religious in high esteem and struggle with the idea of encroaching on their already busy schedule. If you are seeking direction from a layperson, that might not be a factor for you. Yet, lay directors often support themselves via means other than spiritual direction and may also be very busy people.

- We are concerned that the relationship with the potential spiritual director remains positive and healthy (particularly if he is our parish priest or a close acquaintance).

- The process and nature of spiritual growth is an unknown. It is similar to heading into a fog—we are compelled to keep moving, but we don't know what will come of our decision to continue forward. This is particularly true for those who are new on the journey.

- Some of us are worried about the orthodoxy of those who might be available to help us. We want competent guides and are worried that we might be led astray by those who are not faithful to the Church's teachings or who are influenced by New Age or other non-Christian spiritualities. This is a valid concern and all the more reason to ensure we have a solid understanding of our faith, and particularly the Church's teachings on prayer and the spiritual life.

So, the first question is one of motivation. Are you ready to suffer whatever discomfort you may feel for the greater end of finding peace of soul and living life according to your ultimate purpose? If your answer to this question is yes, then half the battle is won. Be encouraged—you are unique in this world; God is calling you and you are listening. Here are some basic ways to overcome these inhibiting emotions and challenges:

1. Increase your knowledge and understanding of the spiritual direction process. You have already made much progress on this point by reading this book. Keep up the good work!

2. If you are still concerned about the faithfulness or perspective of a particular priest or potential director, be direct and don't let this keep you from moving forward.

3. Recognize that the care of souls, as through spiritual direction, is central to the call of a priest and some religious. Any good priest will be encouraged to discover and work with a soul committed to following Christ. Laypersons too, if called to this apostolate, have the same perspective, though they are likely to be employed and occupied by the normal life activities that all of us share who are not priests or religious.

4. Approach the busy schedule of your potential spiritual director with a practical respect. Here's a secret for getting the first meeting or even subsequent meetings set up: Be persistent! Spiritual directors, particularly if they are pastors, are extremely busy. One of the ways spiritual directors practice stewardship with their time is to ensure that those who approach them for spiritual direction take the relationship very seriously. How do they do this? Simply put, they don't make it easy to get an appointment. I am not saying that they will oppose the directee's attempts to meet, but they will gauge the interested directee's constancy as a way to determine how serious they are. At first blush this may sound insensitive. Yet, if you had more demands against your time than you could fulfill, how would you handle the situation? Good directors know that those who persevere in jumping through the hoops necessary to meet with them are likely to take the process seriously. Don't get discouraged if the first and second attempts don't yield the results you want. Be respectfully and gently persistent!

Beyond these items, here's an outline of how to get your first meeting set up and how to ensure that it goes well:

Your First Meeting, Step by Step

1. *Contact your potential director and request a twenty-minute meeting to have a "brief discussion about your spiritual life."* No need to be elaborate here—just short and to the point.

2. *Prepare yourself for the meeting.* Before your first meeting, review the section below entitled "Preparation for Meetings." Ensure that you limit your discussion to very specific spiritual goals or challenges you are facing. For example, you might present something as simple as, "I am struggling with my prayer life." A good director will take it from there and ask you whatever questions they need to know to help you diagnose and overcome the challenges you face.

3. *Work very hard to stay on track.* The best way to accomplish this is to write down the items you wish to review with them. The process of writing or typing out your areas of concern will help you to prayerfully prepare and clarify the specific issues you want to cover.

4. *Arrive before your scheduled time.* Never make your spiritual director wait for you. Remember, the demand for good directors is high. Those directors who are particularly pressed for time will have a corresponding commitment to manage their time well. If you honor that commitment, you are more likely to have a healthy ongoing relationship. Confirm the end time as you begin your meeting to signal your sensitivity to their schedule. You can do this by simply saying, "Thank you for taking the time to meet with me. Just so I am sensitive to your time, it looks like we should end our meeting at 10:00?"

5. *End on time.* Carefully watch the clock, especially if you tend to be gregarious and talkative. If you are obviously sensitive to their schedule, they will recognize that you value their time and will be more open to your next request. If you come in unprepared, and talk on and on, be prepared for difficulty in getting follow-up meetings. I can't emphasize this enough. Excessive rambling indicates to the director that our listening skills and self-awareness are nowhere near what they need to be to allow for effective direction and effective stewardship of the valuable time allotted.

6. *As your time comes to an end, write down and repeat back the direction you received.* Ask your director or potential director, "Have I understood you properly...?" This is not only a very helpful practice but it will indicate to your director that you are serious and are listening—a worthy investment of time.

7. *If all seems to go well, as you wrap up your meeting, ask him or her, "Can I follow up with you later if I have more questions or need further insight?"* Ask your director what would be the best

medium to do that (phone, email, or in person). Sometimes, if the geographical distance between you and your director is significant, you can leverage alternative means to connect with them. Some directors and directees even use web-conferencing tools to do this (e.g., Skype™). That said, it is always optimal to meet face-to-face. Communication between people of goodwill is difficult even when they agree. With the kind of issues discussed in spiritual direction, it is preferable to establish as solid a foundation of understanding as possible. Face-to-face meetings are the best way to do this, especially in the beginning of the relationship.

8. *For subsequent meetings, start off by reviewing what they advised you to do in the last meeting and update them on your progress, questions, difficulties, etc.* This will be another strong signal that you are well worth their effort and time.

9. *Consider offering a donation at the conclusion of the meeting.* It is not unusual to offer at least twenty dollars for a half hour, and some spiritual directors ask for up to sixty dollars per session or higher. Some religious orders and organizations forbid or discourage the spiritual director from asking for a fee. Use your own discretion and be sensitive to the fact that they have given up valuable time to serve you toward Christ—an invaluable gift that deserves our tangible generosity in response. If you are meeting with someone from a religious order, it might be more appropriate to write a check to the order itself. We'll talk more about this later.

10. *If you are convinced that this relationship should be ongoing, don't hesitate to schedule the next meeting then and there, and get a specific date and time.* Don't be shy. On two occasions I have witnessed what I suspect is a common challenge with directors and directees: The directee and director speak of a follow-up meeting, but fail to schedule it because both are caught up in being too deferential to the other. The end result? No meeting! Don't fall into this trap. If this is God's will for

you, then schedule the next meeting—no ifs, ands, or buts about it.

With these tools in hand, your next step is to get on the phone and set up an appointment. Regardless of the outcome, you are being obedient to the call of God. He will reward your courage and diligence and provide what you lack. In due time, I have no doubt that "He who began a good work in you will bring it to completion" (Phil. 1:6).

Facing the Challenge

Sometimes, some of the factors we have discussed along with the work required to grow spiritually will cause hesitation with respect to the pursuit of and participation in spiritual direction. St. Teresa of Avila clearly warns us that those seeking to deepen their spiritual lives will find a great many obstacles in their way. The enemy of our souls dreads nothing more than one who is fully immersed in Christ. Even though this commitment can be difficult, we must be clear and resolute about our need for Christ and the critical assistance that spiritual direction provides us in knowing and following Him. We must be committed to facing these challenges along with those that can be even more difficult to overcome (e.g., self-disclosure), and those that emerge from the depth of damaged souls who know that their only hope is redemption and change in and through Christ.

SPIRITUAL DIRECTOR RESPONSIBILITIES

It is worth reiterating at this point that it is not the responsibility of the spiritual director to manage your spiritual growth. A spiritual director is not a wealthy physician with an office staff and a file for each patient that he reviews before every visit. Quite the contrary, spiritual directors often give their lives to this work for very little monetary compensation if any at all. They are often fully employed elsewhere, or if they are religious or diocesan employees they will have plenty of other assignments to tend to. With this understanding as a backdrop, directors have responsibilities inside and outside of spiritual direction. Thankfully, the Congregation for the Clergy has published an extraordinarily helpful work on this topic entitled *The Priest, Minister of Divine Mercy: An Aid for Confessors and Spiritual Directors.*[14] This book will help both directors understand their responsibilities (particularly priests), and directees gain a better understanding of how the process works from a priestly or spiritual director point of view. Since this topic is not the focus of this book, we will only review a few key responsibilities.

Outside of giving spiritual direction, good spiritual directors should be receiving spiritual direction themselves; they should be growing in their own faith and have active accountability in their lives. Beyond this, they should cultivate virtue, knowledge, and prayer:

Virtue: They should cultivate an energetic, consistent, and systematic pursuit of holiness.

Knowledge: They should have a life habit of responsibly and continually deepening their understanding of the spiritual life, Church teaching, and related issues.

Prayer: They should pray and sacrifice regularly and sincerely for those they direct. In particular, they should have a regular and well developed prayer life.

Within spiritual direction, good directors generally will:

- Remember that they are only instruments of the Holy Spirit and a help to those they direct. Directors should never see themselves as the protagonist of the relationship.

- Be careful to prayerfully listen to the prompting or leading of the Holy Spirit regarding root cause issues hindering the spiritual progress of the directee.

- Strive to listen and understand what the directees really mean, not just what they say.

- Be slow to speak and quick to ask clarifying questions instead of assuming that they understand everything right away.

- Gently but sometimes firmly challenge directees, out of love, to be open, honest, and accountable regarding their commitments, and to be faithful to what God is asking of them.

Admonitions to Directors

Beyond the foundation of these basic attitudes, Jean-Baptiste Chautard, in *The Soul of the Apostolate*, concisely lays out the topics that should be covered in each spiritual direction session. These admonitions are given specifically to directors:

Peace. Find out if the soul has *genuine* peace, not simply the peace that the world gives, or the peace that results from absence of struggle. If it has none, try to give the soul a relative peace, in spite of all its difficulties. This is the foundation of all direction. Calmness, recollection, and confidence also come in here.

A High Ideal. As soon as you have collected enough material to classify the soul[15] and to recognize its weak points as well as its strength of character, temperament, and its degree of striving for perfection, find out the best means of reviving its desire to live more seriously for Jesus Christ and of breaking down the obstacles that hinder the development of grace in it. In a word, what we want here is to get the soul to aim higher all the time.

Prayer. Find out how the soul prays, and, in particular, analyze its degree of fidelity to mental prayer, its methods of mental prayer, the obstacles met with, and the profit drawn from it. What value does it get out of the sacraments, liturgical life, particular devotions, ejaculatory prayer, and the practice of the presence of God?

Self-Denial. Find out on what point, and especially how the particular examen is made, and in what manner self-denial is practiced, whether through the hatred of sin or the love of God. How well is the custody of heart kept? In other words, what amount of vigilance is there in the spiritual combat and in the preserving the spirit of prayer throughout the day?

These are the basic and universal responsibilities of any spiritual director. Spiritual directors are human and imperfect, and a directee might find that a director has strengths and weaknesses in these areas of responsibility. The good news is that if we understand how spiritual direction can and should work, we can help ensure that the process is as fruitful as is possible even with the normal weaknesses that crop up on both sides of the relationship.

Healthy Relational Boundaries

Both the director and directee must ensure that the relationship never crosses appropriate interpersonal boundaries. Aside from the ground covered in the chapter "What Is Spiritual Direction?" it is completely inappropriate for a director and directee to have any kind of physical, sexual, or emotionally dependent relationship. If either party has an objective sense that the relationship is crossing these boundaries, the relationship should be terminated immediately.

One important note is in order here. It is common for a directee to have a healthy transference of affection for their director. It is absolutely normal, for instance, to appreciate someone who is helpful to you—especially in as vital a matter as the spiritual life. This affection is appropriate as long as both parties are able to recognize this natural response and ensure that it remains healthy.

MY RESPONSIBILITIES
IN SPIRITUAL DIRECTION

As indicated in previous sections, directees must take complete ownership of their spiritual growth and the direction process. We considered the idea that spiritual directors are not like physicians who have a staff and computing systems to chart and track those whom they serve. Instead, directees should take on the very responsibilities they often expect their directors to own. Though it may sound strange, it is good to think of yourself as the one who keeps your own chart, journal, progress notes, etc. Unlike a physician, you should be the one to review and prepare your own notes prior to each meeting and to update those notes at the end of each meeting. One aspect of your relationship is similar to that of a doctor-patient relationship: you need to do the work to make and keep regular appointments. Beyond those foundational elements, the following are key aspects of the directee's responsibilities.

Docility and Obedience

Docility is an area of great importance in the spiritual direction relationship and can easily be misunderstood. This is especially true of modern seekers who often recoil at the slightest idea of submission or subjection of one's will to the guidance of another. With modern Western Catholic writers on the topic of spiritual direction you may find strongly stated cautions regarding this issue. Often this is because of sincere sensitivity to abuse and a legitimate concern to ensure that the directee remains totally free to follow or disregard any of the guidance received in direction. In Eastern Church traditions (e.g., Greek or Russian Orthodox), you are more likely to find equally strong statements on the other end of the spectrum. In the East, any directee would be cautioned to avoid spiritual direction if they were not ready and willing to completely open and submit their soul in obedience to another. In the East the sincere concern is that the directee overcome any delusion or self-deception through trusting submission to the judgment of another. In reality, both of the extreme forms of these concerns can result in unintended problems. Simply put, if you are docile to misdirection, you will be misdirected to your own detriment and by your own choice. If you are stubborn toward sound direction, you will misdirect yourself, and likely to great spiritual detriment.

Because of the abuses on the overly submissive side of the spectrum, there is often an equal and opposite over-reaction. As is common with opposite extremes, wisdom resides closer to the middle. The key is that we should always maintain our freedom to act according to our own will in our submission to God, and we should maintain an equal readiness to humbly accept the insight and direction of any director who is worthy of our trust. Here's a little more insight into the ideas of docility and obedience:

Docility. True docility is an essential ingredient in any successful spiritual direction relationship. What is docility? Docility is a humble readiness to follow God's will for our lives. This is sometimes expressed in the willingness to listen to and follow imperfect counsel from an imperfect person, and at times, even when we disagree or don't completely understand. It is critical to remember that we are in spiritual direction because we recognize that the human condition requires outside counsel to grow. The fact that we are finite fallen creatures requires that someone help us to see the areas of our souls that we cannot see without help. Even if our director is wrong on a particular matter (assuming the direction is not something sinful), we will most assuredly benefit from heading down paths that we would not have chosen on our own. This simple exercise of taking unfamiliar paths will reveal things to us that we would have never been able to see without having been prompted to do so.

Obedience. Some writers on the topic of spiritual direction will make a distinction between what they call docility and obedience. Typically, they will point out that obedience is something that occurs only in a slave-to-master relationship when the slave has no will of their own. This approach is often a well-intended overstatement to make the point. It is true that no directee should act in such a way as to substitute the will and desires of the director for their own. It is also true that no directee is, by definition, sinning if they choose to disobey their spiritual director (unless of course their counsel echoes the commands of God himself). Yet, it can be a profound act of holiness to obey your spiritual director, particularly when they are suggesting something that is very difficult but may nonetheless lead us to a deeper relationship with Christ. The key here is to remember that God never usurps our free will; neither should a spiritual director. In a healthy relationship a spiritual director is not able to influence our lives without our consent.

If what we are directed to do is in keeping with God's law as reflected in Church teaching, and we are choosing to obey by our own choice, we are on solid spiritual ground and will likely find great blessings through our obedience. Christ Himself demonstrated this reality as a youth. "He went down with them and came to Nazareth, and was obedient to them.... And Jesus increased in wisdom and in stature, and in favor with God and man" (Lk. 2:51–52).

Openness

More than one thousand years ago, St. John Climacus wrote these words about openness in spiritual direction: "A pilot cannot save a ship on his own without the assistance of his sailors. Nor can a physician cure a patient unless he is entreated...by the sick person who in complete confidence reveals the wound. Those who were ashamed of consulting a physician have left their wounds to fester; often many of them have even died as a result of this."[16] The human condition has not changed since St. John penned this admonition. As a sad illustration of this truth, a family acquaintance recently died of cancer. In discussion about the tragedy of losing a wife and mother with young children, an even more horrifying reality surfaced. The woman *knew* she was sick but would not submit herself to a physician because of her fear. The irony is tragic but very common in the spiritual life. We would often prefer to suffer in our misery than entrust ourselves to someone who might be able to help us. Instead we hide our pain under the cloak of denial while the spiritual cancer eats away at our souls. Some of the best among us cloak this condition through good works, keeping busy by serving the Church and engaging in other positive activities. All the while, the sickness of a particular sin or imperfection chips away at our bridge of grace to God, until one day we turn to find the bridge weak and impassable. Aside from regular participation in the sacraments, the most powerful reinforcement for that bridge of grace is to bare our souls; to open them up to another; to trust that God will give us what we need through them. Without this willingness, spiritual direction is merely another notch on the belt of spiritualized action items that will yield little progress toward securing the great freedom that Christ has prepared for each one of us.

Regardless of what we call our affirmative response to the Holy Spirit within our director's guidance, an attitude of humility is absolutely essential to an effective spiritual direction relationship. Without it, we have simply added another voice to our lives that we can argue with while remaining stuck in patterns that we have long been blind and enslaved to.

Preparation for Meetings

Though we have briefly covered this in a previous section, it is worth digging a little deeper into preparation. Let's look at a simple review of three types of preparation: *remote, proximate, and immediate.*

Remote Preparation

Preparing for your next spiritual direction starts during the last moment of your previous spiritual direction. By making a note of the key insights that you received during direction and by identifying some concrete actions you will work on, you create your own spiritual map for the coming month. You can capture the insights in meaningful phrases like "discouragement never comes from God" or "I am impatient because I am arrogant." You can capture concrete actions in motivational phrases like "I spend the first three minutes of my commute thanking God for today's blessings" or "When I come home, I give the first ten minutes entirely to my wife" or "When my friends start to gossip, I change the topic." Put these phrases in your planner, your journal, your home page—wherever you will be sure to see them regularly. Don't leave spiritual direction without this map. By the way, it is not necessary to invent new points in every spiritual direction; sometimes simply changing a word or two on a previous phrase can refresh it for you, or sharpen it. Also, your insights and concrete actions should be connected to your program of life or your rule of life (we will talk more about this idea later); you should perceive the connection clearly.

Proximate Preparation

The day before your spiritual direction, take some time to sit down and look over the map you made after the last spiritual direction. Asking the Holy Spirit for light, analyze the following areas, making notes where relevant (e.g., I really made progress on this point. I made no progress here, and I am not sure why. This crisis came up and totally derailed me...). Remember, always include the question "Why?" as part of your analysis. The analysis will leave you with things to report and questions to ask. This will be the agenda for your spiritual direction. (Your spiritual director may suggest alterations to the following list; it is meant to be a reference point.)

1. The general state of your soul since last spiritual direction

2. Difficulties or failures in your moral life since last spiritual direction

3. The effectiveness of your desired progress phrases from last spiritual direction

4. Progress on and results of the concrete actions chosen after your last spiritual direction

5. The main points of your plan of life, if they were not covered in 3 and 4

6. Challenges and progress in your prayer life, if they were not covered in 3 and 4

7. The quality of the key relationships and responsibilities of your state in life, if they were not covered in 3 and 4

You will not necessarily have a lot to say to your spiritual director regarding every single one of these points during each meeting. But as you go through them yourself, you will identify those points that you really do need or want to address. This proximate preparation, the calm and prayerful analysis of these areas, is like cleaning out the garage: It refreshes your soul and motivates you to look with enthusiasm towards the coming month of spiritual work.

Immediate Preparation

A few minutes before your spiritual direction, make a visit to our Lord in the Blessed Sacrament to put everything in His hands. If the Eucharist is not nearby, say a prayer to the Holy Spirit to guide you and your director. Make sure you have the notes from your proximate preparation. Finally, call to mind the real goal of all spiritual direction: to discover more clearly God's action in your life and to equip you to respond generously to whatever He is asking of you.

Maintaining Continuity

We all know that infrequent exercise does not do us much good. Conversely, frequent, regular exercise provides a great deal of lasting benefit. This is even truer with respect to participation in the sacraments and spiritual direction. The reason the benefit is greater is that God has chosen these avenues as means of grace for His people. Now, to be clear, the graces received in spiritual direction are not comparable to those God provides through the sacraments. However, good spiritual direction always results in a richer participation in the sacraments of the Church. As with exercise, regularity is critical to develop spiritual momentum and strength. Brief bursts of spiritual fervor rarely result in the peace and fulfillment that Christ makes available for every pilgrim in the Faith.

It bears repeating that often spiritual directors' calendars are so full that it can be difficult to get an appointment. Some directees find this discouraging and get frustrated with their directors. The simple solution is for the directee to own the responsibility of regular meetings. This may require the regular inconvenience of multiple phone calls or emails to get each meeting set up. Rather than being frustrated with this issue, directees need to see this as part of their sanctification and growth in humility and patience. The alternative is a frequency of direction that will yield less positive and inconsistent progress. A good rule of thumb is that directees should meet with their directors approximately once every three to four weeks when beginning the process. Once established, these meetings can move to four to six weeks or once a quarter if all is going as planned.

Financial Matters

Is there any higher endeavor in life than working to conform and submit our souls to Christ? Is there any activity worthy of more attention and energy? How about financial energy in the form of donations?

St. Paul in his first letter to Timothy indicates that those who lead well, with respect to the souls in their care, are worthy of "double honor" (1 Tim. 5:17). This "honor" Paul speaks of is no less than material honor. Yes, our priests and religious are often called to vows of poverty. However, this does not mean that they always have all that they need to live and carry out their respective apostolic work. Laypeople as well who give of their time often do so at the expense of career growth or other pursuits they might enjoy rather than spending their time serving you. Regardless of where the money goes, our generosity is a reflection of the health of our souls, and for the health of our souls we should be *particularly generous* with anyone willing to invest their time in our spiritual well-being. What I am not speaking about here is whether or not directors should charge a fee. My emphasis here is that regardless of whether or not they charge a fee,[17] our disposition should be one of generosity.

That said, financial matters should never, never, never be a barrier to your spiritual growth. There are creative ways to generously respond to the provision and needs of your spiritual director. Do they have a non-financial need that you have the means to meet? Are you a CPA, mechanic, or a chiropractor? Does your director need any of these services if you are unable to assist financially? If there is no material way to support them, then it is always prudent to offer a specific commitment of spiritual sacrifice on their behalf (e.g., a decade of the Rosary a day, etc.).

I CAN'T FIND ONE, NOW WHAT?

Well, if you are not face-to-face with God yet, your striving for whatever God has called you to is not finished. As astute readers can tell by this point in the book, the process of self-evaluation, preparation, and seeking are almost as important as the spiritual direction relationship itself. If you are struggling to find a good director, or experiencing a poor quality of direction, be of good cheer; you are in good company! St. Teresa of Avila also experienced this particular challenge. In her autobiography she laments having to endure the misdirection of a number of poor spiritual directors over about a twenty-year period. Yet her deep commitment to this practice never waned. She continued seeking directors until she encountered several who offered life-changing perspectives on prayer and sanctity. What did she do in the mean time? She kept striving, kept looking, and remained active and committed to her pursuit of Christ.

So, what is the answer for us? Keep looking, keep striving, keep seeking, and keep working on yourself as best you can. As with St. Teresa, Christ will meet you in your seeking and help you to advance as you should even without a spiritual director (if that is His will for a time). In the meantime, keep reading this book and offer up a prayer to St. Joseph, as St. Teresa advised us: "Those who cannot find a master to teach them prayer should take this glorious Saint for their master, and they will not go astray."[18]

SPIRITUAL PROGRESS INSIDE AND OUTSIDE OF SPIRITUAL DIRECTION

Spiritual direction can be likened to a good rearview mirror and a clean windshield. The rearview mirror provides a healthy perspective of what lies behind us; the windshield, a clear view to what lies before us. All of these gifts of perspective, hope for the future, and spiritual progress can come in a powerful way in and through the process and personal encounters of spiritual direction. To ensure the best possible visibility on this exciting journey to God, there are a handful of exercises and tools you will find helpful before and during your travels. With respect to the spiritual life, the challenge for many is that they don't recognize the need for a clean windshield, a clear rearview perspective on the past, or side-view mirrors to help with blind spots. Those who do recognize the need still exercise various levels of skill in using these tools, or fail to use them at all (like those who choose not to use seatbelts). When we first sat behind the wheel of a car, training was necessary to ensure successful navigation and safe travel. Regarding the importance of these tools, many of us had to learn the hard way through minor and sometimes major accidents, or near accidents. In the same way, there are tools in the spiritual life that are very helpful for safe and effective travel.

After interviewing a number of experienced spiritual directors, the use or lack of use of one particular tool distinguishes whether or not the spiritual direction relationship is one that is quite effective or somewhat less effective. Said another way, there are some directees who experience a great deal of growth in spiritual direction, and some who struggle more and experience far less benefit in the process. Believe it or not, the simple distinction between the two is often whether or not they take advantage of spiritual exercises.

What is it about spiritual exercises, a silent retreat, or any kind of guided spiritual retreat that has such a significant impact on spiritual growth? It really is very simple. Spiritual retreats provide an environment where the directee gains a much more heightened awareness of their own spiritual state. It is a place where they can escape the incessant noise that has become normal in our society. Only in a state of quiet reflection can we begin to really hear the voice of God and evaluate our lives in a meaningful way.

Accordingly, the following exercises are best pursued during some kind of silent retreat. Many have had their lives deeply changed through Ignatian spiritual exercises or similar retreats. Regardless of what form you choose, without setting time aside (even if you can only manage to be alone in your car for a few hours), the prayerfulness, insights, and perspectives most helpful in these exercises will be limited at best. You already take your spiritual life seriously; don't sell yourself short in this process.

If you are unable to attend a retreat, the next best option is to set aside several hours on a weekend. Find a local Church where you can sit before the Blessed Sacrament in silence. Then, spend as much time as you can in that sacred silence. Think about your life, about your death, about what will happen when you see God face-to-face. Will he say, "Well done"? Will you be ashamed? Will you be joyful? Will you suffer? Sit in silence and invite the Holy Spirit to help you evaluate your life. But, before we venture into the silence, there is a very important relationship that can and should help us on our way.

MARIAN DEVOTION AND
THE SPIRITUAL LIFE

The aspect of spiritual development that is most mysterious to me is Marian devotion. On this topic I will offer a more personal observation. During my conversion to Catholicism, the doctrines concerning Mary were among the most difficult to embrace. The turning point was when someone pointed out several things to me. First, they challenged me to reflect on the Scripture passage in Romans 13 where St. Paul instructs us to "give honor to whom honor is due" (v.7). Then they posed a simple question: "If we are called to give honor to whom honor is due, and the Archangel under God's command gives honor to Mary, then we are honoring God if we reflect that same disposition." A corresponding conclusion I came to was that if we are honoring God by honoring Mary, then we are not in any way robbing God of devotion due Him; we are in fact giving Him our worship by doing so. Shortly after my conversion I decided, though it was difficult at first, to begin giving honor to whom honor was due. Since that time my devotion to Mary has remained steady, and I believe that Mary's intercession has been critical in my own growth.

Beyond my own experience, spiritual masters have consistently pointed to the invaluable assistance of the Mother of God in helping us to know and love Christ. I have found this to be a profound reality best captured by the beautiful hymn entitled "Mary the Dawn" by Father Justin Mulcahy, CF:

Mary the dawn, Christ the Perfect Day;

Mary the gate, Christ the Heavenly Way!

Mary the root, Christ the Mystic Vine;

Mary the grape, Christ the Sacred Wine!

Mary the wheat, Christ the Living Bread;

Mary the stem, Christ the Rose Blood-red!

Mary the font, Christ the Cleansing Flood;

Mary the cup, Christ the Saving Blood!

Mary the temple, Christ the Temple's Lord;

Mary the shrine, Christ the God adored!

Mary the beacon, Christ the Haven's Rest;

Mary the mirror, Christ the Vision Blest!

Mary the mother, Christ the mother's Son.

By all things blest while endless ages run.

Father Garrigou-Lagrange, in his book *The Three Ages of the Interior Life*, sums up Mary's role effectively:

> When the bases of the interior life are considered, we cannot discuss the action of Christ, the universal Mediator, on His mystical body without also speaking of the influence of Mary.... Many persons delude themselves maintaining that they reach union with God without having continuous recourse to our Lord who is the way, the truth, and the life. Another error would consist in wishing to go to our Lord without going first to Mary.... Protestants have fallen into this last error. Without going as far as this deviation, there are Catholics who do not see clearly enough the necessity of having recourse to Mary that they may attain to intimacy with the Savior. Blessed Grignion de Montfort speaks even of "doctors who know the Mother of God only in a speculative, dry, sterile, and indifferent manner; who fear that devotion to the Blessed Virgin is abused, and that injury is done to our Lord by honoring too greatly His Holy Mother...." They seem to believe that Mary

is a hindrance to reaching divine union. According to Blessed Grignion, we lack humility if we neglect the mediators whom God has given us because of our frailty. Intimacy with our Lord in prayer will be greatly facilitated by true and profound devotion to Mary.[19]

Father Lagrange completed this great work on the spiritual life just one year before "Blessed Grignion" (whom most people know as St. Louis de Montfort) was canonized. St. Louis de Montfort is a master of wisdom regarding devotion to Mary and is, as of the writing of this book, a candidate to become a Doctor of the Church. In *True Devotion to Mary*, St. Louis reveals much more about development of the interior life and devotion to Mary. Here are two key passages from this great work that are well worth reflection:

Take notice, if you please, that I say the saints are molded in Mary. There is a great difference between making a figure in relief by blows of hammer and chisel, and making a figure by throwing it into a mold. Statuaries and sculptors labor much to make figures in the first manner; but to make them in the second manner, they work little and do their work quickly. St. Augustine calls our Blessed Lady "the mold of God"—the mold fit to cast and mold gods. He who is cast in this mold is presently formed and molded in Jesus Christ, and Jesus Christ in him.[20]

The third good which Our Lady does for her servants is that she conducts and directs them according to the will of her Divine Son. Rebecca guided her little Jacob, and gave him good advice from time to time; either to draw upon him the blessing of his father, or to avert from him the hatred and persecutions of his brother Esau. Mary, who is the Star of the Sea, leads all her faithful servants into a safe harbor. She shows them the paths of eternal life. She makes them avoid the dangerous places. She conducts them by her hand along the paths of justice. She steadies them when they are about to fall; she lifts them up when they have fallen. She reproves them like a charitable mother when they fail; and sometimes she even lovingly chastises them. Can a child obedient to Mary, his foster-Mother and his enlightened guide, go astray in the paths of eternity? "If you follow her," says St. Bernard, "you cannot wander from the road."[21]

Finally, wrapping up the wise reflections of Fr. Lagrange and St. Louis, St. Teresa of Avila has also encouraged recourse to Mary and the saints, particularly in the battle of spiritual development:

They must take his Blessed Mother and his saints as intercessors that these intercessors may fight for them.... Truly in all states it's necessary that strength come to us from God.[22]

SPIRITUAL SELF-EVALUATION

My Spiritual Heritage

The first exercise is to write out a brief description of your spiritual journey in order to increase your awareness of God's presence and work in your life. One way to do this is to take a few pieces of paper and create sections for each major period of your life. For example, age 0–9, then outline the period of 10 to 18, then from 19 to 25, and so on. It doesn't matter how you organize each period of time or exactly how you divide it out. What matters is that you highlight key moments that have significance in your spiritual journey. For the time you lived with your parents, jot down the key elements of their spiritual influence. It may be helpful to recall any history you know about their spiritual journeys. What were their beliefs about God? How did they live? What did they tell you about God? What did their lives tell you about God? What were the subtle or unwritten rules about faith in your home? What were the overt beliefs about faith? As we reflect on these, we need to seek to understand the connections to our attitudes, beliefs, dispositions, and struggles with our own faith.

Next, express any spiritual inclinations or non-inclinations you may have had during these periods (or the next as it best applies). When did you first think about God? What was your life like from the standpoint of virtue, strengths, or weaknesses? Remember that these are just the highlights (we are not looking for a complete autobiography here). Once you complete this rearview-mirror look at your life, move into the present and begin by asking yourself what has triggered your current interest in spiritual direction or the desire to move deeper into your relationship with God.

My Spiritual Status

This next step is critical and relates the current state of your spiritual life. Take a minute and indicate where you find yourself in each of these foundational areas of your faith-habits and faith-life. As you review and write notes regarding these items, beware of any temptation to excessive self-criticism or scrupulosity. Always keep in mind that the spiritual life is a journey of a thousand steps. For people of goodwill, at every point in the process, no matter how holy or unholy we think we are or were, we will always find potential areas of improvement and progress. The key is to remember to be patient and take the process one step at a time.

My Relationship with Christ

How would I describe my relationship with Christ? Is it "personal"? Is Jesus far away from me, or does He seem very close to me? Am I aware of His presence constantly or only in very rare situations? Is my faith a matter of duty, or is it an expression of love and devotion? Do I serve God out of fear, or am I compelled out of an overwhelming sense of gratitude? Regardless, be careful not to condemn your status in any way. Fear, for instance, is a good beginning point and one that reflects the standing of many as they launch deeper into their faith. Don't worry about the goodness or badness of any position on the spectrum. The key is simply to identify *where you are now* so that you can effectively move forward in your spiritual quest.

My Sacramental Participation

What is the frequency of my participation with sacraments of the Church and other aspects of worship?

	Daily	Weekly	Monthly	Quarterly	Annually	Other/ Don't Know
Eucharist/ Mass						
Adoration						
Confession						

My Prayer Life

What is the state of my prayer life?

	Daily	Weekly	Monthly	Quarterly	Annually	Other/ Don't Know
Vocal Prayer (Rosary, other formula prayers)						
Mental Prayer						
Examination of Conscience						
Other						

What form(s) of prayer do I enjoy most and why?

What form(s) of prayer do I struggle with the most and how?

Do I struggle with prayer in general? If yes, in what way(s)?

My Spiritual/Intellectual Development

What is the state of my spiritual reading or intellectual development of my faith?

I read...	Daily	Weekly	Monthly	Quarterly	Annually	Other/ Don't Know
Scripture						
Spiritual books						
Theological, apologetics/ other Catholic materials						

My Root Sin
What Is It?

What is your root sin? If you are new to the process of spiritual direction, this question might strike a strange chord with you. What is a "root sin" after all, and why does it matter? In older writings on the spiritual life you might come across this idea of root sin called "ruling passion," "predominant fault," "dominant defect," or "dominant passion." Regardless of what we call it, if you understand the phrase, "getting to the root of the problem," then you have the basic idea.

When there are problems at the *root* of a tree, these problems often manifest themselves in the *fruit* of the tree (or in the lack of fruit). The condition of the fruit is merely a symptom of the condition in the roots. The fruit of an unhealthy tree will manifest symptoms that point to problems with the roots of the tree. To solve the problem, we must recognize the symptoms in the fruit and then deal with the roots.

Similarly, we experience many symptoms or fruits of root sins. We might be irritable, impatient, intolerant, unhappy, etc. Though we may confess these things or the most serious manifestations of them, we often fail to understand the root problems or root sins behind them. If we limit our problem solving to a focus on symptoms, we are not likely to get to "the root of the problem" and really find a meaningful solution. This is sometimes why Catholics of goodwill can find themselves frequently falling into and confessing the same serious sins over and over again. So, the value of root sin identification is in diagnosing and solving the root problem (or the real problem), instead of wasting our time focused on the symptoms.

Depending upon which spiritual tradition we draw from, there are many ways to classify, categorize, and understand root sins. The *Catechism of the Catholic Church* provides an overview of the definition and classification of sins beginning in paragraph 1846. For our purposes we will keep this as simple as possible and provide three basic categories of root sin—pride, vanity, and sensuality—that are given in a traditional exposition of 1 John 2:16.

A note about progressive evaluation might be helpful here. When we begin the work of a serious commitment to holiness, we will discover that the field (the soul) that we desire to plow and plant is riddled with rocks (sins) that need to be removed in order to make progress. At this point of discovery, the faithful spiritual farmer begins to remove these big obvious rocks (usually mortal sins). At some point the farmer becomes satisfied with this effort, pulls the plow out of the shed and sets out to prepare the soil, but then is startled at a disconcerting discovery: Though all the big rocks are gone, there are many more rocks that are smaller (venial sins) that had not been seen before. The big rocks had properly drawn all of the attention. Now that the big rocks are clear, a more detailed and sometimes more rigorous effort is then needed to further prepare the field. The same is true with the progressive nature of root sin identification and clarification as we grow in spiritual maturity.

To help with this challenge, instead of beginning with a detailed analysis of the traditional seven capital sins or some other more complex examination, with the assistance of Fr. Bartunek we have instead provided a simpler list of three. I am confident that this approach will be more than sufficient to get the big rock removal effort started. In our experience, these three categories will serve the spiritual farmer well into initial healthy spiritual development and even into more mature stages. Under the guidance of good spiritual reading and a director, once the reader determines that a more rigorous evaluation is necessary, they should then pursue the rich resources recommended in this book and those on the website to guide their efforts to plow more challenging terrain.

How Do I Identify My Root Sin?

This is where it can get even more problematic when working alone. Self-diagnosis is both challenging and often dangerous. As an example ,there can be many causes of severe chest pain. As you can imagine, the appropriate determination of the root issue of this kind of pain is absolutely critical. The pain may only be a symptom of muscle strain or heartburn. You can readily guess what happens when someone is suffering from potential heart failure and they take an antacid instead of going to the emergency room. No one with a healthy desire to live a long life would ever leave serious symptoms like these to self-diagnosis. Wise people who experience serious chest pains get themselves into a physician as quickly as possible. Why? Because the doctor is trained to evaluate symptoms in a way that allows them to identify the root issue, the real cause, and to thereby treat it efficiently and effectively.

Similarly, it can be very difficult, challenging, and potentially perilous to attempt self-diagnosis in the most critical areas of our lives—the state of our souls. The challenge of diagnosis is even more difficult in our spiritual lives. Why? Because medical illnesses do not have active willful agents behind them. What I mean by this is that sin often brings temporal benefits to the sinner. A genetic disposition to heart disease is simply a bodily defect without intent. Sin is a serious illness that often is nurtured by intent and disordered desire. Even worse, it is in the best interest of the enemy of our souls to keep deceiving us in these matters. In the parable of the sower and the seed, Jesus clearly reveals the active work of the devil to deceive and keep us from the truth.

"When anyone hears the word of the kingdom and does not understand it, the evil one comes and snatches away what is sown in his heart" (Mt. 13:19).

Even so, just as we can do our own medical research and get a good general idea of what we need, we can make progress on our own (especially as we have the promise of the guidance of the Holy Spirit in John, chapter 14). Sometimes physicians and medical researchers will provide self-evaluation checklists that potential patients can review before seeing a physician. In the case of root sin identification, we've provided a self-diagnosis review and checklist below. This effort can at least get us started in the right direction as we begin or seek to further improve our spiritual growth. You still need objective feedback of your assessment by your spiritual director. Father Lagrange admonishes us to ask ourselves:

"What does my director think of this? In his opinion, what is my predominant fault?" No one, in fact, is a good judge in his own case; here self-love deceives us. Often our director has discovered this fault before we have; perhaps he has tried more than once to talk to us about it. Have we not sought to excuse ourselves? Excuses come promptly, for the predominant fault easily excites all our passions: it commands them as a master, and they obey instantly. Thus, wounded self-love immediately excites irony, anger, impatience. Moreover, when the predominant fault has taken root in us, it experiences a particular repugnance to being unmasked and fought, because it wishes to reign in us. This condition sometimes reaches such a point that, when our neighbor accuses us of this fault, we reply that we have many bad habits, but truly not the one mentioned.[23]

As Lagrange rightly counsels, it is wise to accept the observations of our spiritual director or a trusted friend. If our first instinct is to reject their perspective, we might find upon a second and honest look that they are right and our reaction is a self-protection mechanism that needs to be overcome. Of all the exercises in this book, the admonition for external input is a strong one. This can't be over-emphasized because the human person has an infinite capacity for self-deception.

Root Sins and Their Manifestations

The following is a list of three root sins and some of their most common manifestations provided by Fr. John Bartunek. We have also included several warm-up questions to get you thinking in the right direction. This process should be handled with a great deal of prayer and simplicity. First, just as with the previous exercises, be sure that you are in a quiet place (most preferably with Christ in adoration). Second, pray and ask the Holy Spirit to give you insight and wisdom and ensure that you sit in silence before the Lord for a few moments before you begin. Be careful not to get caught up in the wording of the questions or examples and to avoid any tendency to split hairs. If you don't understand a particular statement or question, just move on. Also take caution to avoid any concern over the less than perfect distinction between root sins. The human heart rarely works in perfectly clear distinctions of vice and virtue. The goal in this exercise is to be approximately right versus precisely wrong. Because of our fallen human nature, all three root sins are present in all of us, but one usually predominates. Identifying that one is the goal of this exercise. Begin your exercise with one of these prayers:

> Lord, help me to see the obstacles in me that get in the way of my growth in love and service to you and others. Help me to see the things that I have chosen that keep me from you. Help me to see the things that I may have not deliberately chosen that keep me from you. Help me to be honest with myself and see clearly where you desire to set me free and then help me to

be courageous and ruthless in rooting out the darkness and allowing your light to heal me and draw me firmly onto the path of life. Amen.

Oh blessed Trinity, help me to know my deeds and myself without deception or duplicity. Save me, dear God, from falsehood and pretension, not only in the eyes of others but also in the depths of my soul. I am weak and faulty. Make me grow strong, holy, and honest with pure intention. I ask with grace to know the clarity of how I have sinned, how I have failed you and others. Most particularly I beg to know the roots and reasons and sources of my sins to begin to see myself as I really am. To acknowledge the deep flaws and weakness of character that lie under the surface of my behavior. What kind of person am I? Oh God, tell me, tell me unsparingly. I wish to listen to you with all humility. Help me to be led by you to live a better and more holy life. Lord, help me also to be completely sorry once again for all the ugly, hateful, and unspeakable past evil of my life. You and I know what that wretched evil has been. Make me sorrier for it than I have ever been before. Come, O Holy Spirit, fill my mind with light and my heart with honesty. Immaculate mother of Christ and honest St. Joseph, please pray for me and help me. Amen.

Next, prayerfully and slowly review your warm-up questions (provided below). Write down your brief reflections on each. Then, begin your review of the root sin manifestations. If you have seen any of the manifestations in yourself, simply check them off upon your first pass through. Complete your first pass quickly. Check the manifestations even if they ring true only in the slightest sense. Then, once you have completed your first pass, stop and pray again. Sit in silence again for a time. Pray and ask the Holy Spirit to guide you. Then take a second turn back through the warm-up questions and the checklist. This time work more slowly through the checklist and put a star next to those symptoms that most frequently appear in your life. You should begin to notice more stars or checkmarks appearing in one of the three root sin categories. This is the place to begin your next battle against sin in your life. Be encouraged! The Holy Spirit, through this exercise, is leading you into a new phase of progress and growth.

Root Sin Evaluation Warm-up Questions:[24]

1. To what do my thoughts naturally tend? What are the preoccupations of my heart? What keeps me up at night? Where do my thoughts and desires spontaneously take me when I am alone or without distractions?

2. What is generally the cause or source of my sadness, my anxiety, my frustration, my lack of peace, my joy, or my pleasure?

3. When I have knowingly sinned or disobeyed God, what was the sin or what was my motivation to sin? What are the patterns of sins that show up regularly in confession? Is there a sin or an issue that I regularly bring up in confession?

4. If and when I have resisted or avoided God in any way, how have I done so? What was at the bottom of my motivation? Why did I do it? What temporal benefit did I gain from the resistance or avoidance?

Root Sin of Pride

Pride: Excessive love of one's own excellence or desired excellence. Pride manifests itself when we seek our self-worth and security in our own abilities, traits, or strengths

Never	Sometimes	Frequently	Focus	Manifestations of the Root Sin of Pride
				1st Review: Move quickly and assess by instinct. If you hesitate, go with your first instinct.
				2nd Review: Review items checked in Sometimes or Frequently categories. Determine manifestations that require attention and identify them in Focus column with a checkmark.
				too high an opinion of myself or an elevated concept of myself
				annoyance with those who contract me or question what I say
				inability to submit to those who I judge as less competent or less spiritual than I am

Spiritual Self-Evaluation

Never	Sometimes	Frequently	Focus	Manifestations of the Root Sin of Pride
				Manifestations of the Root Sin of Pride *1st Review: Move quickly and assess by instinct. If you hesitate, go with your first instinct.* *2nd Review: Review items checked in Sometimes or Frequently categories. Determine manifestations that require attention and identify them in Focus column with a checkmark.*
				refusing or resisting assent to others without a satisfactory explanation
				anger if I don't get my way or am not taken into account
				easily judgmental, putting others down, gossiping about them
				slow to recognize or acknowledge my own mistakes or weaknesses
				slow to see when I hurt others and and inability to seek and give forgiveness
				frustration or anger when others don't thank me for favors or work that I do
				unwillingness to serve, rebellion against what I don't like or agree with
				impatience, distance, brusqueness in my daily contact with others
				thinking I am the only one who knows how to do things right
				unwillingness to let others help me or advise me
				inflated idea of my own intelligence and understanding
				dismissing what I do not understand or what others see differently
				not feeling a need for God, even though I do say prayers
				nursing grudges, even in small matters
				never taking orders or bristling when orders are given to me
				inflexible in preferences or perspective
				always putting myself and my things first
				indifference towards others and their needs, never putting myself out for them
				centering everything (conversation, choices, recreation, etc.) on myself and my likes
				calculating in my relations with God and with others

Root Sin of Vanity

Vanity: Excessive concern for and seeking our security in how we are perceived (what others think about us)

Never	Sometimes	Frequently	Focus	**Manifestations of the Root Sin of Vanity** *1st Review: Move quickly and assess by instinct. If you hesitate, go with your first instinct.* *2nd Review: Review items checked in Sometimes or Frequently categories. Determine manifestations that require attention and identify them in Focus column with a checkmark.*
				always seeking admiration and praise, worrying about not getting it
				excessive concern about physical appearance
				dedicating excessive time to "primping" one's person or possessions
				hoping "I am the best" and finding ways to get others to think so
				being guided by the opinions of others rather than principle
				some types of shyness out of fear of not being liked/accepted by others
				sacrificing principles in order to fit in
				placing too high a premium on popularity and acceptance
				easily discouraged at my failures
				hypocrisy or two-facedness in order to be accepted
				taking pleasure in listening to gossip
				taking pleasure in hearing about or speaking about others' failures or misfortunes
				breaking confidences
				stretching the truth or outright lying to be admired or to hide shortcomings
				severe disappointment when others don't appreciate my ideas or possessions
				always wanting to be the center of attention, at times stretching the truth or lying outright, or being uncharitable in my words in order to achieve this

Root Sin of Sensuality

Sensuality: seeking our security and self-worth in possessions, comfort, or the avoidance of discomfort (real or perceived).

Never	Sometimes	Frequently	Focus	Manifestations of the Root Sin of Sensuality
				1st Review: Move quickly and assess by instinct. If you hesitate, go with your first instinct. *2nd Review: Review items checked in Sometimes or Frequently categories. Determine manifestations that require attention and identify them in Focus column with a checkmark.*
				laziness
				always seeking comfort, that which requires the least effort
				not going the extra mile for others
				procrastination, last minute in everything
				shoddiness, complaining, excessively affected by minor discomforts
				inability to sacrifice
				not doing my part at home
				always expecting everyone else to serve me
				behavior and decisions ruled by my feelings and moods instead of my principles
				daydreaming a lot with self at the center
				unable to control my thoughts when they attract me, even when they are not good
				doing or partaking in only what I enjoy (food, drink, work, etc.)
				allowing what I enjoy or prefer to push out what I should do
				uncontrolled curiosity, wanting to see/experience everything
				senses and impulses overrule what I know is right and wrong
				acting out feelings (frustrations, desires, etc.) with no regard for God or others
				only working with those I like, being easily hurt
				fickleness and inconsistency
				unable to stay on track without constant supervision
				can never finish what I start

The "No" and "Yes" of Real Spiritual Growth

Now that you have completed this exercise and have a reasonable guess as to the identification of your root sin, there are a few questions worth further consideration. Is identification of one's root sin enough to experience real spiritual growth? Is it enough to just say "no" to our root sins? Is it enough to experience sorrow and then to exercise resolve in resisting our root sin?

On the topic of true and false repentance St. Paul says:

"Now I am glad: not because you were made sorrowful; but because you were made sorrowful unto penance. For you were made sorrowful according to God . . . For the sorrow that is according to God worketh penance, steadfast unto salvation; but the sorrow of the world worketh death. For behold this selfsame thing, that you were made sorrowful according to God; how great carefulness it worketh in you" (2 Cor. 7:9–11, Douay-Rheims).

St. Paul points out here two different types of sorrow in reaction to sin. One of them brings life to the soul; the other leads to despair and spiritual death (sometimes even physical death, as in the case of suicide). As we evaluate our root sins and examine the state of our souls before God, there are two paths we can follow. The first path is one of "the sorrow of the world" or what we will call an incomplete repentance. What I mean here by "incomplete" is the idea that it is not enough to merely recognize our sin or even to experience remorse about it. We also need to reject it, turn away from it, and choose a new path. An incomplete repentance is one that only achieves recognition of sin and destructive behavior but nothing else.

The second path of repentance is the true or complete path. On the second path we recognize our sin before God and therefore, in light of His unlimited mercy and love, we experience true godly sorrow. This contrition in turn leads to real and complete repentance that includes, at minimum, confession and penance. In the Gospel of Matthew, Jesus provides chilling insight into what is required to move from a position of the recognition of sin to one that reflects complete repentance.

> *"When an unclean spirit goes out of a person it roams through arid regions searching for rest but finds none. Then it says, "I will return to my home from which I came." But upon returning, it finds it empty, swept clean, and put in order. Then it goes and brings back with itself seven other spirits more evil than itself, and they move in and dwell there; and the last condition of that person is worse than the first" (Mt. 12:43–45).*

Though this passage falls within the broader context of God's relationship with Israel, it also reveals a spiritual principle that clearly has personal implications. In this passage, Jesus allows us to look beyond the veil of the flesh and into the spiritual reality of a kind of sorrow that is destructive to the soul. He helps us to see that a true turning to God involves more than just recognizing and saying no to sin and appetites of the flesh. In fact, He reveals that an incomplete repentance is a very dangerous spiritual state.

So, how do we know that our repentance is complete or incomplete? How can we avoid the error of identifying and ridding ourselves of a particular sin and then potentially finding ourselves in an even worse position afterward? John the Baptist provides the answer in Matthew, chapter three. Here the prophet of God is calling Israel to repentance and baptizing them for the forgiveness of sins. As he sees the most prominent practitioners of faith in his day approaching him, he rebukes them for their arrogance and show of religion and challenges them to "produce fruit as evidence of your repentance" (v.8). St. Catherine of Sienna in her Dialogue 49 brings this to an even finer point: "It is not enough for eternal life to sweep the house clean of deadly sin. One must fill it with virtue that is grounded in love."

So what then is complete repentance? What is the sorrow of God that leads to life, salvation, peace, and spiritual growth? What is it that we need to do (by the grace of God) to avoid the incomplete repentance that Christ reveals leaves us in a state of vulnerability to greater sin?

True repentance has three parts: one, the recognition of and sorrow for sin; two, turning away from sin (if we are on the right path, the first two stages bring us to the sacrament of confession); and three, doing good works that reflect a turning away from particular sin. A note of clarification is in order. The third stage of repentance includes whatever penance that emerges out of confession, but also then extends more fully into our lives as we walk in grace "and produce fruit as evidence of our repentance." In fact, the grace we receive in the sacrament of penance is often the very thing we need to effectively battle sin and live out virtue!

So, in identification of our root sin through the previous exercise we have laid the groundwork of a real and substantive turning toward God in our repentance. In the next section we will outline a practical approach regarding how to exercise a complete repentance and avoid the perilous scenario Jesus described above. As you explore these ideas it is critical to note that without Christ we are not able to see ourselves clearly or find the way to eternal life. The good news is that the call to holiness is not a command that we execute on our own as a sheer act of will; the command also comes with a promise of mercy and aid.

In his letter to the Ephesians, St. Paul, inspired by the Holy Spirit, writes these comforting words that not only point us to the grace of God but also to the fact that He has already prepared the path of holiness before us:

"But God, who is rich in mercy, out of the great love with which he loved us, even when we were dead through our trespasses, made us alive together with Christ (by grace you have been saved), and raised us up with him, and made us sit with him in the heavenly places in Christ Jesus, that in the coming ages he might show the

immeasurable riches of his grace in kindness toward us in Christ Jesus. For by grace you have been saved through faith; and this is not your own doing, it is the gift of God—not because of works, lest any man should boast. For we are his workmanship, created in Christ Jesus for good works, which God prepared beforehand, that we should walk in them" (Eph. 2:4–10).

Beyond Sin to Virtue and Holiness

You must give up your old way of life; you must put aside your old self, which gets corrupted by following illusory desires. Your mind must be renewed by a spiritual revolution so that you can put on the new self that has been created in God's way, in the goodness and holiness of the truth (see Eph. 4:22–24). The New Testament is replete with examples of this same type of exhortation. The basic pattern can be simplified this way: Turn *from* sin (whatever that sin may be), and turn *to* virtue (whatever that virtue may be).

This is the exact outline we are advocating here. You have identified your root sin; now it is time to identify the opposite virtue. If we purposefully, clearly and specifically identify the opposite virtue, the *narrow path* of *complete* repentance becomes obvious and practical. This narrow path is the same path to which Jesus alluded when he said:

> *"Enter by the narrow gate; for the gate is wide and the way is easy, that leads to destruction, and those who enter by it are many. For the gate is narrow and the way is hard, that leads to life, and those who find it are few" (Mt. 7:13).*

If this is still feeling a bit vague, the following diagram and description of the process may be helpful.

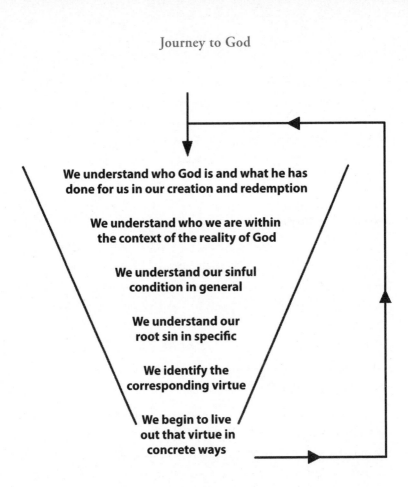

We understand who God is and what he has
done for us in our creation and redemption

We understand who we are within
the context of the reality of God

We understand our sinful
condition in general

We understand our
root sin in specific

We identify the
corresponding virtue

We begin to live
out that virtue in
concrete ways

First, as we pursue God and the Church, the sacraments, prayer, Scripture, study, and spiritual reading, we begin to understand Him better. We discover how much He loves us and we discover what He's done specifically for us as individuals. We find help in the context of our need and struggles of day-to-day life. This awareness, then, naturally leads to a shift in our understanding of who we are. Our identity then begins, at least in our own awareness, to take shape within the context of who God is and how He is working, loving, living, and breathing within us. I say "in our own awareness" not because this is a reality that we manufacture but because it is a reality we begin to see and understand in a tangible and personal way. As we move deeper into this relationship, by the work of the Holy Spirit, we begin to see how it is that we are succeeding and struggling in our efforts to deepen that relationship. We understand what pleases Him. We understand those things within us that hinder or damage our friendship and intimacy with Him.

At some point those who are working diligently on their spiritual lives begin to see patterns of sin and patterns of virtue. They begin to recognize what God is asking of them (frequently, this is when the faithful pilgrim seeks out spiritual direction) and rejoice in what God is doing in and through them!

So, as illustrated above, we identify our root sin and then identify the corresponding virtue that we desire to cultivate and use to push our root sin out of our lives. We then work to concretize our pursuit of virtue on a week-to-week, day-to-day, and hour-to-hour basis. Finally, the process begins all over again, until we see Him face-to-face and hear, "Well done, good servant!" (Lk. 19:17).

To specifically tie our discussion back to Jesus' reference to the narrow path, this diagram, this process, this life rhythm, *is* the narrow path. Even more specifically, the path of virtue and practicing virtue in the context of grace and a vibrant relationship with Christ is the narrow path that leads to life, joy, and peace in Christ. In St. John's Gospel Jesus said, "The thief comes only to steal and kill and destroy; I came that they may have life, and have it abundantly" (10:10). Living a life of virtue and grace with and in Christ is an abundant life and is the life replete with gifts of grace that only the diligent pilgrim can know!

Identifying the Corresponding Virtue

Ultimately we are seeking to live a *positive* life of virtue; *not* one focused on sin or our and is the life replete with gifts of grace that only the diligent pilgrim can know failures. Though beginners in the spiritual life will often be required to focus on the elimination of habitual sin, the process as a whole should be a positive, active, living path, not a negative one.

Said another way, facing and overcoming sin is like coming to a fork in the road of our spiritual lives. We are confronted with the choice regarding a particular sin and we choose to either stay on the narrow path or take the path of destruction, away from God. Assuming the course we've chosen is toward God, once we have identified and confessed our sins, that fork in the road is then behind us as we pursue God and holiness down the narrow path of virtue. We live a life-orientation that readily recognizes that a particular sin or imperfection is behind us and God is with us and before us. Jesus' admonition in Luke 9:62 is apropos:

> *"No one who puts his hand to the plow and looks back is fit for the kingdom of God."*

St. Paul echoed this same thought when he said in his letter to the Philippians (3:13b–14):

> *"Forgetting what lies behind and straining forward to what lies ahead, I press on toward the goal for the prize of the upward call of God in Christ Jesus."*

It is critical therefore to focus the vast majority of our energy on the forward pursuit of virtue, not on the sins, sinful inclinations, or attachments of the present or the past. Our sin can and will provide the sign posts on our path that help us identify the battles we are called to fight on the narrow way leading to God. Yet it should never be the primary focus of our energy.

For example, a hypothetical directee shares that she struggles with a specific manifestation of vanity. She enjoys the trophies, awards, and praise related to her accomplishments so much that she would constantly seek to draw a great deal of attention to her achievements. In this case her director helped her to identify that the proper path of virtue was to focus specifically on helping others to succeed, avoid any effort to take credit, and ensure that she gave proper accolades to others in the process. She also determined that she should solve problems and serve others without in any way revealing that she had done so, and rather than letting her friends know what charities she had given to, she determined that she should make quiet, anonymous donations and contributions.

So let's break this down, the way she and her spiritual director would, in her specific plan, to deal with this hindrance to her spiritual growth:

Root Sin: Vanity

Manifestation: When I accomplish anything good, I am always looking around for praise. Sometimes I fail to acknowledge the contribution of others in my work. At times I have gone so far as to stretch the truth regarding my real accomplishments.

Opposite Virtue(s): Modesty and Humility

Plan of Action Toward God

- I will meditate on and memorize a passage of scripture on the humility of Christ as expressed in Philippians, chapter 2.

- I will pray the humility prayer every day in the morning for at least the next thirty days.

- I will examine my conscience at the end of each day and write down my failures and successes in following this plan. I will thank and praise Him for my successes and ask forgiveness for my failures.

- I will review my daily notes with my spiritual director at the end of each week.

- I will go to confession if I stray too far off this path.

Plan of Action Toward Others

- I will do at least one work of charity each day and specifically avoid telling anyone under any circumstance. I will not even hint at the good I have done.

- If my good works are noticed, I will say, "Only by His grace" and purposefully change the subject to cast light on something good accomplished by someone else.

A few observations are in order. First, we need to be as specific as we can in our commitments to pursue virtue and avoid sin. Without this specificity, it is very difficult to determine if we are successful or not at the end of each day. To the degree we are specific, we will be accountable; to the degree we are accountable, we will be humble and dependent; to the degree we are humble and dependent, we will receive the grace we need to overcome sin and exercise virtue. Second, there are no cookie-cutter formulas available for this soul cleansing. Our souls are more unique and different from one another than are our faces. Every battle, though it has similarities to those experienced by others, is unique to us as individuals. Each person needs to outline a plan that is customized to their situation under the guidance of the Holy Spirit and a holy spiritual director.

Living Virtue on a Day-to-Day Basis

As we observed, one of the secrets to success in this area lies in getting as specific as is possible. If you struggle achieving a practical specificity, ask yourself a few key questions, beginning with:

If I were to explain my root sin to someone who didn't know me very well, how would I do it?

Now, after you think about this for a moment, stop and write down your explanation in the context of the categories below:

What is my root sin? How does it specifically manifest itself in my daily life?

- *Toward God?*
- *Toward myself?*
- *Toward others?*

Then, do the same for the corresponding virtue:

If I were to explain my desire to live out a particular virtue in a specific way, how would I do it?

Now, after you think about this for a moment, stop and write down your explanation:

What is the virtue I desire to live out? How might it specifically manifest itself in my daily life? When my day is done, how will I know if I have specifically and tangibly lived out this virtue? At the end of the day, what questions can I ask myself to determine if I have lived out my commitment?

- *Toward God?*

- *Toward myself?*

- *Toward others?*

The answer to these questions will now serve as an examination of conscience that you can use on a periodic basis to evaluate your progress and review the outcomes with God and your spiritual director.

Obviously there are thousands of combinations of manifestations of sin and their corresponding virtues. These are just a few examples. If you get stuck, the best way to get creative insight on sin and virtue is through part three of the *Catechism of the Catholic Church* entitled "Life in Christ," and in particular, articles seven and eight.

NAVIGATION ON
THE NARROW PATH

The good thing about a narrow path is that the narrowness provides clarity regarding the way we should go. I believe this is one of the reasons that Jesus said, "My yoke is easy and my burden is light" (Mt. 11:30). The spiritual life is really one of simplicity and ease once we get beyond the initial stages of growth (which we will explore in a moment). When we encounter complexity regarding the choices we face, we need to be cautious. The difficulty is often related to an unholy attachment to particular aspects of our decision or some other factor related to our concupiscence. When we walk simply and resolutely with our God, the path before us is simple, light, and marked by a predominant peace. Yes, Jesus did say that the path to Him is one of self-sacrifice and cross-bearing, but we must remember that the vast majority of difficulty comes from our own sin and need for purification, not because of God's arbitrary imposition of difficulty upon us.

As we navigate this path, there are a number of helpful signposts that can help us to determine if we are on the right track. So far, much of this book has focused on helping you to develop self-knowledge, an essential element on the spiritual journey. Keep in mind, however, that awareness of God is our ultimate goal. Self-knowledge, in the light of God, is only the beginning of any meaningful growth in our relationship with God. These initial steps lay the groundwork for the rest of our journey. We can never expect to plot an accurate course to our destination if we don't know where we stand at the start.

The other value of self-knowledge is that it provides a kind of internal alarm or GPS system to warn us if we are off track. If we know who God is, and where He is, or what His will is, and we know who we are and where we are in the process of spiritual growth, we can more easily recognize when we've gone off course and get back on track much quicker. As with all stages of our journey, the rich traditions of the Church provide us with invaluable guideposts and insights to keep us on the right path. As we begin to wrap up this handbook we will look to an understanding of the spiritual life that the Church has developed over the past two thousand years: the three ways.

THE THREE WAYS OF
THE SPIRITUAL LIFE

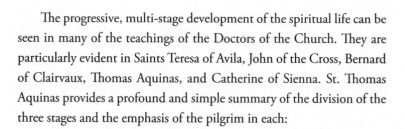

The progressive, multi-stage development of the spiritual life can be seen in many of the teachings of the Doctors of the Church. They are particularly evident in Saints Teresa of Avila, John of the Cross, Bernard of Clairvaux, Thomas Aquinas, and Catherine of Sienna. St. Thomas Aquinas provides a profound and simple summary of the division of the three stages and the emphasis of the pilgrim in each:

> The first duty which is incumbent on man is to give up sin and resist concupiscence, which are opposed to charity; this belongs to beginners, in whose hearts charity is to be nursed and cherished lest it be corrupted. The second duty of man is to apply his energies chiefly to advance in virtue; this belongs to those who are making progress and who are principally concerned that charity may be increased and strengthened in them. The third endeavor and pursuit of man should be to rest in God and enjoy Him; and this belongs to the perfect who desire to be dissolved and to be with Christ.[25]

Though these and other saints did not always use the terms we commonly use to describe these phases today, they clearly taught using analogies that reflect commonly experienced phases of maturity that serious Christians work through in their progress to God. These phases are predominantly classified as "purgative," "illuminative," and "unitive"—words that focus on what happens at each stage. Because of their obscurity, however, we often employ another set of terms that signify the spiritual maturity of a person at each phase: "childhood," "adolescence," and "adulthood" (we will use these terms interchangeably):

Phase 1: Purgative Way (Childhood)

Phase 2: Illuminative Way (Adolescence)

Phase 3: Unitive Way (Adulthood)

Common Challenges Along the Ways

Before we review the definition and characteristics of these phases, we should look at a number of common challenges that surface when we attempt to identify a phase in our spiritual growth.

The first error is scrupulosity. It is not healthy to obsess about our exact location on our spiritual journey. God is the only one who will ever know exactly where we are at each point and, as St. Paul said, in this life we can only "see now through a glass in a dark manner" (1 Cor. 13:12, Douay-Rheims). We sometimes need to squint a bit and do the best we can. For this purpose the Holy Spirit has graciously provided unique insights to these phases through the writings of various saints throughout the ages. Still, we need to exercise caution as we seek this wisdom so as not to be tempted to imbalance by our own disordered affections, self-obsessed curiosity, or by the enemy of our souls.

One of those to whom God did reveal many great truths of the spiritual life is St. John Klimakos. He portrayed progress in the spiritual life as moving up thirty steps of a ladder. In his work, each step calls for a particular approach to cooperating with God in our spiritual maturation. As you can imagine, this kind of specific insight could be very beneficial, and it has been to many for centuries. On the other hand, Father Eugene Boylan, in his wonderful work, *Difficulties in Mental Prayer,* said this about the common challenge of obsession with identifying too specifically which stage one finds oneself in:

> It is by no means necessary, at least as a general rule, to know on which rung one is standing. The important thing is to avoid standing still and to keep on climbing.[26]

Father Boylan's point is very wise and obviously flows from a good deal of reflection and experience in the direction of souls to Christ. As he rightly points out, and in no way contradicts St. John's wisdom, the primary benefit of thinking through the idea of these phases is to ensure that our course is right and that our momentum is constant. These two factors are far more central than the perfect identification of any specific location within the three ways.

This first error, obsession with an overly specific *location* in spiritual maturity, is the mother of a second common error: assuming that progress through these phases is perfectly linear as if moving up the steps of a ladder. In reality, though the spiritual Doctors of the Church agree that that there are identifiable stages of maturation in the spiritual life, they also agree that getting through these stages is a messy affair on a practical, day-to-day level. If our ascent was a linear and perfectly ordered step-by-step process, that would be a dream! Unfortunately, because of our wayward tendencies and the complexities of our fallen nature, we constantly stumble, leave the path, take diversions, and then fight our way back on track. On the more positive side, a non-linear ascent may also be a result of our unique design and the restless love of the Holy Spirit within us! St. Teresa of Avila, St. Catherine of Sienna, and other spiritual masters have noted several other factors that can confound us in our ability to properly identify the "you are here" status of our spiritual lives:

- In His grace and wisdom, God can choose to elevate someone at an unexpected or uncommon pace. This reality can catch both the spiritual director and the directee off guard. Both need to be alert not to hinder the work of the Holy Spirit when uncommon or supernatural growth does occur.

• Early on in spiritual development, it is common for God to encourage us through favors that may last only briefly. These consolations can sometimes be misunderstood as evidence that we are far more advanced in the spiritual life than we actually are. Any mystical experiences should always come under the scrutiny of a spiritual director—this will protect the pilgrim from common attempts at deception from the enemy and self-deception that can easily lead them astray.

• The pilgrim can experience isolated or common characteristics that reflect participation in *several* phases at once. This can be particularly difficult and confusing for the directee. However, any solid spiritual director should be able to help the directee understand where they are in their journey even when things might be foggy to the directee.

• The enemy of our souls can often attempt to distract us through religious experience that mimics the real thing, or, by tempting us to focus on legitimate experience. This is a common and dangerous trap that often leads to spiritual pride. I have had the opportunity to engage with a number of well-intentioned "mystics" who were obsessed with their experiences and who would not take direction to divert their attention away from these experiences and towards service to God and neighbor. The refusal to set aside experience is a clear sign that something is amiss.

A third error is to think that this progression leaves something behind, as if it were a journey along a path up a spiritual mountain. This problem can surface with the use of any term like "phase." For instance, as we enter into the purgative (childhood) phase, we begin the most basic practices of vocal prayer and the purposeful purging of habitual sin from our lives. Regardless of how far we are in our spiritual progress, we should never completely leave these practices behind. We will never mature out of the benefits of vocal prayer or regular confession. Though the spiritual journey can be likened to a mountainous adventure, when we climb a mountain we leave terrain behind us, but we still need support for the way ahead that we find above us (and that comes from the ground covered behind us!).

So, from a visual representation standpoint, the phases might be better thought of as foundations for one another in the same manner as the construction of a multi-story building. As we move from the first to the second floor, we require that all the structure of the first floor remain intact. As we realize the benefits of the second floor, we do so only because the graces, virtues, or spiritual practices of the first floor remain stable, present, and ever-growing in strength. Still, the building analogy only serves to illustrate that the foundational elements never lose their importance. However, as with the ladder analogy, if we take these concepts too far and view the stages as distinct floors in a building where we are either on one floor or another, but never both at once, then the imagery can be confusing.

A fourth challenge is with our own vacillation between phases. This problem becomes clearer when we reflect on comparable elements of the spiritual journey that we receive progressively through the life stages of childhood, adolescence, and adulthood. At what point do we leave behind what we were as adolescents and become adults? Do we ever leave *all* that we were behind? Though there is clearly a difference between the stages in retrospect, an exact point of distinction is very difficult to identify when we are in the in-between phases of development. In fact, as we move from adolescence to adulthood, we think and act in ways during that transition that reflect both stages. So, as a nineteen-year-old, we may make both the mistakes of a teenager *and* the good decisions of a mature responsible adult. Both of these acts can occur at the same time in the same person.

For a helpful and practical application of these ideas and boundaries, it is far better to be *approximately right* than *precisely wrong*. As with the root sin identification, we are looking for the most predominant patterns of our progress or regress in the interior life and the life of virtue. As Father Boylan revealed, it is far more effective to understand the general direction of our journey than it is to obsess over each mile marker on the way.

Finally, one more analogy might be helpful. Consider our own education experience. When we were in first grade, we knew very little, though at the time we were learning a great deal. Our education that year was foundational for the second grade and beyond. Some of us learned the alphabet in the first grade. Later, when we were working on our final year of high school, we were still using the same alphabet we learned in first grade (though at a much more mature level). Another way to view this is by spending some time looking back on the entirety of our education from first grade to the present. We will observe that we literally learned millions of lessons between then and now. We learned about history, language, geography, mathematics, writing, speaking, sports, and science. We traveled through this path of learning in a way that shared a common approach (grade levels), but that was unique to our own learning pace, style, imagination, emotions, etc. So although the general path of education was one shared by many, our specific journeys had a million nuances that were unique to us, as well as similarities shared only by those who chose the same career or vocation.

Regardless of when and what we learn in the spiritual life, (1) never see the basic or fundamental practices as unimportant (e.g., vocal prayer and regular confession); and (2) ceaselessly strive to develop a deeper and more intimate relationship of love with God and others.

The Doorway to the Interior Life

Before we get to summary descriptions of each phase of spiritual progress, we should answer an important question: Is there something, some action, some disposition, or some state that will tell us that we have actually entered into the ways, or what is called the interior life of God? The answer is unequivocally yes. St. Teresa of Avila provides this answer in her great work, *Interior Castle*. Here Teresa describes the soul as a Castle with seven primary rooms, each reflecting a different level or manifestations of prayer, virtue, and on the path to union with God.

I thought of the soul as resembling a castle, formed of a single diamond or a very transparent crystal, and containing many rooms, just as in heaven there are many mansions. If we reflect, sisters, we shall see that the soul of the just man is but a paradise, in which, God tells us, He takes His delight. What, do you imagine, must that dwelling be in which a King so mighty, so wise, and so pure, containing in Himself all good, can delight to rest? Nothing can be compared to the great beauty and capabilities of a soul; however keen our intellects may be, they are as unable to comprehend them as to comprehend God, for, as He has told us, He created us in His own image and likeness.

As this is so, we need not tire ourselves by trying to realize all the beauty of this castle, although, being His creature, there is all the difference between the soul and God that there is between the creature and the Creator; the fact that it is made in God's image teaches us how great are its dignity and loveliness.

It is no small misfortune and disgrace that, through our own fault, we neither understand our nature nor our origin. Would it not be gross ignorance, my daughters, if, when a man was questioned about his name, or country, or parents, he could not answer? Stupid as this would be, it is unspeakably more foolish to care to learn nothing of our nature except that we possess bodies, and only to realize vaguely that we have souls, because people say so and it is a doctrine of faith. Rarely do we reflect upon what gifts our souls may possess, Who dwells within them, or how extremely precious they are. Therefore we do little to preserve their beauty; all our care is concentrated on our bodies, which are but the coarse setting of the diamond, or the outer walls of the castle.

Let us imagine, as I said, that there are many rooms in this castle, of which some are above, some below, others at the side; in the centre, in the very midst of them all, is the principal chamber in which God and the soul hold their most secret intercourse. Think over this comparison very carefully; God grant it may enlighten you about the different kinds of graces He is pleased to bestow upon the soul. No one can know all about them, much less a person so ignorant as I am. The knowledge that such things are possible will console you greatly.[27]

Shortly thereafter Teresa comes to answer our question about entry into this beautiful castle. "Insofar as I can understand the door of entry to this castle is prayer and reflection."[28]

So, here we have the two basic elements necessary for entry into the castle:

1. **Prayer.** The *Catechism of the Catholic Church* (2559) reveals the essence of prayer to be "the raising of one's mind and heart to God." As you might suspect, a clear entry into the castle is not necessarily reflected by a fleeting "Dear Lord!" gasped just as we miss that near accident on the highway. No, St. Teresa is talking about a door that we *enter*, not one that we glance at or peek into. Entering this door is an act of commitment to enter into an active relationship with Christ. While we may not understand all that this entails upon our entry, one thing is clear: entering this door of prayer reveals a commitment to pursue God in a manner that we may have likely never before expressed in our lives, a way that reflects substantial, consistent effort and persistence through inevitable trials and setbacks.

2. **Reflection.** The reflection we speak of here is a key component of many of the topics we have covered in previous sections of this book, and in fact is the purpose behind all of the self-evaluation exercises. Reflection is the practice of thoughtfully

and purposefully seeking to understand ourselves with respect to both the glory of God within us and the results of the fall and sin on our present path to God. The end of healthy reflection is always increased self-awareness, increased humility, and deepened gratitude for the great work of salvation that God has and continues to work in us. If our reflection results in anything less, then we are merely exercising a shallow, narcissistic overview rather than an in-depth, God-ward evaluation. A God-ward evaluation will always lead us deeper into union with God.

Entering the door of this castle, beginning the journey of the interior life, is to enter into the first way, the purgative way, the way of spiritual childhood.

Spiritual Childhood

A danger here is to consider spiritual childhood as a negative. In fact, Jesus said that in order to seek the kingdom of God, we must be "born again" (John 3:3–5) and "unless you turn and become like children, you will never enter the kingdom of heaven" (Mt. 18:3). This spiritual childhood is essentially a rebirth into the life of God and grace. Recognizing that we are spiritual children properly places us in the spectrum of this grace and helps us to begin to understand what it means to desire in ourselves the simple love of a child as we grow in love and service to God.

Spiritual childhood or the purgative way presupposes a birth into the life of Christ through baptism. Between our baptism and our entry into the interior castle, there is commonly a state that may reflect a lack of concern for matters pertaining to spirituality, faith, to God, to virtue, and to self-giving. This state is marked by habitual mortal and venial sin, self-centeredness, or a general apathy to matters of eternal significance. There are many reasons why people become pilgrims on the trek into the great depths of God's love. Considering your interest in spiritual direction, the likelihood is good that you have at least passed from spiritual birth into spiritual infancy.

One final preparatory thought is in order. In a previous section we reviewed the idea of complete repentance. The astute observer upon exploring these phases will recognize that the general process of turning from sin toward God, along with growth in prayer, is the process that brings a person into spiritual infancy and through the beginning and subsequent phases of spiritual growth. In fact, this discussion is merely another way to understand the narrow path of the abundant life that Christ calls us to when He says through St. Peter, "Be holy, for I am holy" (1 Pet. 1:16, Douay-Rheims).

In order to better understand each of these sections and help the reader to self-diagnose their current state, we have adapted and modernized wisdom from a helpful work entitled *The Soul of the Apostolate* by Jean-Baptiste Chautard. In each section we will provide a brief definition of the three phases of the spiritual life and then follow these with Chautard's sub-categorization and related characteristics commonly found in each.[29]

Here's an illustration that lays out how the three ways and Chautard's sub-categories fall into place. The three ways—purgative, illuminative, and unitive—are represented on the left of the growth cycle. The seven sub-categories and their relationships to the three ways fall within the lifecycle on the right. You will also notice that the pre-purgative sub-categories of "Hardened in Sin" and "Surface Christianity" do not appear in this illustration for reasons noted in our upcoming exploration of Pre-Spiritual Childhood.

Unitive
  VII: **Complete Sanctity**
  VI: **Heroic Perfection**

Illuminative
  V: **Relative Perfection**
  IV: **Fervor**

Purgative
  III: **Sustained Piety**
  II: **Intermittent Piety**
  I: **Mediocre Piety**

Readers who have never had the opportunity to study mystical or ascetical theology will find a number of terms and ideas summarized here that are likely to be unfamiliar. Terms used in mystical theology often carry very different definitions and nuance than the common-use definitions of the same words. As an example, in chapter eight of *Ascent of Mount Carmel*, St. John of the Cross discusses the difference between contemplation of the intellect and contemplation proper to mystical theology. There is a chasm between these two meanings that is often invisible to the inexperienced traveler, and confusion in this case is easy to come by. To mitigate these difficulties, we have provided an extensive glossary of terms in the appendix. It would be well worth the effort (if you have not already done so) to briefly review the glossary before digging into the next section.

Self-Diagnosis of Your Current Spiritual Progress

As with root sin identification, try to avoid treating this exercise like you would a personality test (such as those frequently found in the workplace). Spiritual status and growth has eternal consequences and our eternal destiny is at stake. If, by God's grace, we fight sin and pursue virtue unto death, we will find Him in all His glory after our purification (if necessary). If we depend on this grace to pursue and love Christ with all our heart, soul, mind, and strength, the same end will come. However, if we fail to fight the good fight, and willingly leave the narrow path or make choices that take us off track, we can expect nothing less than having to face the consequences of our choices. Understanding who we are and where we are in light of our final destination is critical.

To illustrate the serious nature of having a proper understanding of our own spiritual state, the Gospel of Matthew reveals the unhappy end of people that have made a radical misdiagnosis in this regard. Here Jesus takes us on a fast-forward journey to the day of judgment when there were some who came confidently before God and were shocked by His response. "Not everyone who says to me, 'Lord, Lord,' shall enter the kingdom of heaven, but he who does the will of my Father who is in heaven. On that day many will say to me, 'Lord, Lord, did we not prophesy in your name, and cast out demons in your name, and do many mighty works in your name?' And then will I declare to them, 'I never knew you; depart from me." (Mt. 7:21–23). Here Jesus reveals people who acknowledge Him as "Lord" and who do good works by the power and authority of Christ but who are nonetheless in an improper relationship to God—so much so that Jesus reveals that they end up experiencing rejection at their final judgment! How can this be possible? It is possible because people rely on a shallow self-assessment of the state of their souls that results in a perpetual and sometimes spiritually fatal self-deception.

Therefore, we should not take this work lightly. As with our root sin evaluation, it would be best to pursue this exercise during or after a silent retreat (even better if before the Blessed Sacrament in the same context). Whatever we do, we can't sell ourselves short and treat our magnificent souls and the great love that God has given us with anything less than honor and careful respect.

With respect to practical matters, the best way to pursue this self-evaluation is with—you guessed it—a spiritual director. If you have been unable to identify a director, work with someone who takes their spiritual life seriously, or someone who knows you very well (they've seen the real you), to assist you in making this assessment so that it is no longer a purely personal or isolated exercise that will likely be subject to some measure of self-deception.

To get the most out of this exercise on your own, or with help, here are a few steps you can follow:

1. Spend time in prayer and ask the Holy Spirit to help you. This prayer may be helpful:

   Oh blessed Trinity, help me to know my deeds and myself without deception or duplicity. Save me, dear God, from falsehood and pretension, not only in the eyes of others but also in the depths of my soul. I am weak and faulty. Make me grow strong, holy, and honest with pure intention. I ask with humility to know the clarity of how I have sinned, how I have failed you and others. Most particularly I beg to know the roots and reasons and sources of my sins to begin to see myself as I really am. To see the good you have accomplished in me, but also to acknowledge the deep flaws and weakness of character that lie under the surface of my behavior. What kind of person am I? Oh God, tell me, tell me unsparingly. I wish to listen to you with all humility. Help me to be led by you to live a better and more holy life. Come, O Holy Spirit, fill my mind with light and my heart with honesty. Immaculate mother of Christ and honest St. Joseph please pray for me and help me. Amen.[30]

2. Next, if you have not already done so, now is the time to review the glossary of terms so that you are able to clearly understand what the words mean.

3. Then, read the spiritual phases through completely one time. During this reading, underline those elements that seem to accurately reflect your current status.

4. Now take a second pass but do so more carefully and prayerfully. If you think that any item is even possibly present in you, highlight it (if you have not already done so).

5. On the third and last pass, identify the phase that has the most markings—this will be a good start at identifying your relative location in the spiritual journey.

Even with the glossary of terms, you might find some of the ideas difficult to understand in practice. This is where a spiritual director is an invaluable resource to fine-tune your "You Are Here" status and then to help you understand what you need to do to continue to deepen your relationship with Christ.

Pre-Spiritual Childhood

The pre-infancy phase outlined here is not commonly identified in mystical or ascetical theology. The reason for this is that the soul at this stage has yet to enter the interior life in any meaningful way. Chautard identifies two states that reflect those who have yet to reach spiritual childhood or the purgative way. For each state, "Hardened in Sin" and "Surface Christianity," he provides the dispositions or condition of the heart with respect to sin, prayer, sacraments, and imperfections (which we will explain later). It is likely that readers will find themselves beyond these stages; even so, it is helpful to review them and watch for signs of regression during our spiritual journey.

Hardened in Sin

- Mortal Sin: Stubborn persistence in sin either out of ignorance or because of a warped or severely underdeveloped conscience.

- Prayer: Deliberate refusal to have recourse to God for any manner of help or provision.

- Sacraments: Rarely attends Mass, if at all, and does not participate in confession.

Surface Christianity

- Mortal Sin: Considered an insignificant nuisance and easily forgiven. The soul gives way to and commits mortal sin at every occasion or temptation. Confession, if practiced, is almost without remorse.

- Prayer: Mechanical and either inattentive, last on the list of priorities, or easily abandoned by minor distractions or difficulty. These souls rarely enter into themselves in prayer, or do so superficially, and do not set aside or protect specific time for prayer on a daily basis.

- Sacraments: Sporadically attends Mass and confession—often only at Easter and Christmas.

Spiritual Childhood (The Purgative Way)

Our entry into this first phase of the interior life begins with the most basic motivations to pursue God or a meaningful spiritual life. The nascent motivations that bring us to this point are often rooted in fear and duty rather than love and devotion. Even though imperfect, these motivations coupled with perseverance can provide a healthy foundation for pilgrims seeking to deepen their faith. In this phase the will is still very weak and prone to fall into sin. In this phase we also regularly find energetic converts and reverts who have discovered or rediscovered their need for a deeper life of faith. The properly aimed soul in this phase seeks to gain an awareness of its sins, deal with sorrow for past sins, and cultivate a strong desire to rid themselves of these offenses against God and neighbor. Accordingly, we begin to see here the initial efforts at prayer and piety.

Let's look at these characteristics in a bit more detail. Here we will explore three stages: (1) Mediocre Piety; (2) Intermittent Piety; and (3) Sustained Piety, along with their manifestations in the areas of sin, prayer, and the sacraments.

Mediocre Piety

- Mortal Sin: Weak resistance. Rarely avoids near occasions of sin, but seriously regrets having sinned, and makes adequate confessions.

- Venial Sin: Considered insignificant and even at times embraced or desired. Hence the lukewarm state of the will. Does nothing whatever to prevent venial sin, or to pay attention enough to avoid it, or to uncover and uproot it when it is less conspicuous.

- Prayer: From time to time, prays well but still in an ad-hoc fashion. Spiritual fervency is inconsistent and fleeting. Prayer is far from habitual but is valued, even if minimally so. Prayer is usually either intermittently attentive vocal prayer or a petition-based prayer focused on temporal needs and desires.

- Sacraments: Attends Mass regularly and pursues confession more frequently.

Intermittent Piety

- Mortal Sin: Loyal resistance. Habitually avoids the near occasion of sin. Deeply regrets sin when recognized. Does penance to make reparation.

- Venial Sin: Sometimes deliberate. Puts up a weak fight. Sorrow is only superficial. Makes an examination of conscience, but without any method, preparation, or coherence.

- Prayer: Practices vocal prayer regularly. Not yet firmly resolved to remain faithful to structured meditation (time, place, topic, and material). Gives up as soon as dryness is felt, or as soon as there is business to attend to.

- Sacraments: Attends Mass weekly and pursues confession at least quarterly.

Sustained Piety

- Mortal Sin: Never. At most very rare and only when taken suddenly by surprise and then, often it is to be doubted if the sin is mortal. It is followed by ardent feelings of guilt and a desire for penance.

- Venial Sin: Vigilant in avoiding and fighting it and rarely deliberate. Intense sorrow, but does little by way of reparation. Consistent particular examen, but aiming only at avoidance of venial sin.

- Imperfections: The soul either avoids uncovering them so as not to have to fight them, or else easily excuses them. Approves the thought of renouncing them, and would like to do so, but makes little effort in that direction.

- Prayer: Consistently faithful to specific time and approach to prayer, no matter what happens. This prayer includes vocal prayer and meditation that is often affective. Alternating consolations and dryness, the latter endured with considerable hardship.[31]

- Sacraments: Always attends weekly and daily Mass if able. Pursues confession on a regular schedule.

Much of the content of this section and this book as a whole will aid any serious pilgrim to progress in and through the purgative way as described here. Well-formed spiritual directors are often familiar with the most helpful tools required (i.e., approach to prayer, diagnosis of root sin, self-knowledge, etc.) for the maturation of pilgrims in each stage of the journey. Though the specific means of progression through these stages is not the emphasis of this book, if followed diligently, the reader will at least have a good idea of what is necessary for a fruitful journey. Now we will briefly explore spiritual adolescence.

Spiritual Adolescence (Illuminative Way):

This soul in spiritual adolescence is characterized by purposeful and consistent growth in prayer, virtue, love of neighbor, a deeper awakening of the mind and heart in the ways of God, and an increasingly clear understanding of God's will as it applies to a particular state of life. At this point, the struggle to overcome habitual sin, both mortal and venial, and resulting increase in moral stability has, for the most part, been won. The soul has an ever-deepening desire for the heights of union with God and purity in thought, word, and deed. This phase is often preceded or occupied with significant suffering and purifications. However, the soul is also comforted with consolations and favors from God that sustain it through difficult times. It is also common to find mystical phenomena beginning to emerge here. The properly aimed soul in this phase (as illustrated in St. Teresa of Avila's third mansion) longs to avoid offending "His Majesty, even guarding themselves against venial sins; they are fond of doing penance and setting aside periods of recollection; they spend their time well, practicing works of charity toward their neighbors; and are very balanced in their use of speech and dress and in the governing of their households—those who have them."[32]

To better understand this phase we will use two stages of progress from Chautard with minor modifications: (1) Fervor and (2) Relative Perfection.

Fervor

- Venial Sin: Never deliberate. By surprise, sometimes, or with imperfect advertence. Keenly regretted and serious reparation made.

- Imperfections: Wants nothing to do with them. Watches over them, fights them with courage and diligence in order to be more pleasing to God. Still, imperfections are sometimes accepted, though regretted at once. Frequent acts of renunciation. Particular examen aims at perfection in a specific virtue.

- Prayer: Vocal and mental prayer is constantly practiced and gladly prolonged. Prayer is often affective and the prayer of simplicity begins to emerge. Alternation between powerful consolations and fierce trials.

- Sacraments: Fervently participates in weekly and daily Mass if able. Pursues confession at least on a monthly basis. Imperfections are offered in confession for the purpose of obtaining the grace necessary to overcome them (i.e., devotional confession).

Relative Perfection

- Imperfections: Guards against them energetically and with much care and love. They only happen with half-advertence.

- Prayer: Habitual life of prayer, even when occupied in external works. Thirst for self-renunciation, annihilation, detachment, and divine love. Hunger for the Eucharist and for Heaven. Graces of infused prayer, of different degrees. Often passive purification.

Spiritual Adulthood (Unitive Way):

The principle feature of spiritual adulthood is a simple and constant awareness of God's presence and an obvious and habitual conformity to God's will. Here we find deep and abiding joy, a constant love for God and others, profound humility, freedom from the fear of suffering often accompanied by a strong desire to suffer for God, and apostolic fruitfulness. The suffering in this phase is more closely related to joining in the sufferings of Christ for the purposes of His redeeming grace rather than suffering for one's own sins. All of the virtuous developments previously acquired in the soul are assumed present here thus the distinctions are simple. Here we have the final two stages of Caussade's categorization, Heroic Perfection and Complete Sanctity.

Heroic Perfection

- Imperfections: Nothing but the first impulse.

- Prayer: Supernatural graces of contemplation sometimes accompanied by extraordinary phenomena. Pronounced passive purifications. Contempt of self to the point of complete self-forgetfulness. Prefers suffering to joys.

Complete Sanctity

- Imperfections: Hardly apparent and rare.

- Prayer: Frequently experience the transforming union.

As we discuss these latter stages, it is easy to become increasingly mystified by what the terms mean and how they might be practically understood. This common challenge has only one remedy—experience. Any struggles related to understanding these latter stages are of no concern: God will supply whatever insight is necessary for the stage of the present moment. Why then talk about it? Because there is benefit to knowing that there is always a "deeper" level that God is calling us to until the day we see Him face-to-face. St. Teresa makes the argument in the *Interior Castle* that we all need to understand that these deeper levels exist and that they are possible as a fundamental necessity of our own growth.

As we conclude this exploration, it is worth noting that the vast majority of pilgrims will likely find themselves somewhere within the purgative way. If the drawbridge and door into the purgative way is prayer and a God-oriented self-knowledge (through reflection), the guarantee of passage is in perseverance and the grace of God (who promises to give Himself liberally to those who strive for holiness). St. Teresa of Avila in her powerful illumination of this place of spiritual growth revealed that getting through the purgative way[33] can be a challenge that requires steadfast determination. In the second mansion of *Interior Castle,* she provides a critical admonition that we have here preserved with minor adaptations in italics to enhance clarity.

This chapter has to do with those who have already begun to practice prayer and who realize the importance of not remaining in the first *dwelling places,* but who often are not yet resolute enough to *move beyond these rooms deeper into the castle,* and will not avoid occasions of sin, which is a very perilous condition. But it is a very great mercy that they should contrive to escape from the snakes and other poisonous creatures, if only for short periods and should realize that it is good to flee from them. In some ways, these souls have a much harder time than those in the first *rooms*; but they are in less peril, for they seem now to understand their position and there is great hope that they will get farther into the castle still....

These souls, then, can understand the Lord when He calls them; for, as they gradually get nearer to the place where His Majesty dwells, He becomes a very good Neighbour to them. And such are His mercy and goodness that, even when we are engaged in our worldly pastimes and businesses and pleasures and haggling, when we are falling into sins and rising from them again (because these creatures are at once so venomous and so active and it is so dangerous for us to be among them that it will be a miracle if we escape stumbling over them and falling)—in spite of all that, this Lord of ours is so anxious that we should desire Him and strive after His companionship that He calls us ceaselessly, time after time, to approach Him; and this voice of His is so sweet that the poor soul is consumed with grief at being unable to do His bidding immediately, and thus, as I say, it suffers more than if it could not hear Him.

I do not mean by this that He speaks to us and calls us in the precise way which I shall describe later; His appeals come through the conversations of good people, or from sermons, or through the reading of good books; and there are many other ways, of which you have heard, in which God calls us. Or they come through sicknesses and trials, or by means of truths which God teaches us at times when we are engaged in prayer; however feeble such prayers may be God values them highly. You must not despise this first favour, sisters, nor be disconsolate, even though you have not responded immediately to the Lord's call; for His Majesty is quite prepared to wait for many days, and even years, especially when He sees we are persevering and have good desires. This is the most necessary thing here; if we have this we cannot fail to gain greatly. Nevertheless, the assault which the devils now make upon the soul, in all kinds of ways, is terrible; and the soul suffers more than in the preceding *dwelling places;* for there it was deaf and dumb, or at least it could hear very little, and so it offered less resistance, like one who to a great extent has lost hope of gaining the victory. Here the understanding is keener and the faculties are more alert, while the clash of arms and the noise of cannon are so loud that the soul cannot help hearing them. For here the devils once more show the soul these vipers—that is, the things of the world—and they pretend that earthly pleasures are almost eternal: they remind the soul of the esteem in which it is held in the world, of its friends and relatives, of the way in which its health will be endangered by penances (which the soul always wants to do when it first enters this *dwelling place*) and of impediments of a thousand other kinds.

Oh, Jesus! What confusion the devils bring about in the poor soul, and how distressed it is, not knowing if it ought to proceed farther or return to the room where it was before! On the other hand, reason tells the soul how mistaken it is in thinking that all these earthly things are of the slightest value by comparison with what it is seeking, faith instructs it in what it must do to find satisfaction; memory shows it how all these things come to an end, and reminds it that those who have derived so much enjoyment from the things which it has seen have died. Sometimes they have died suddenly and been quickly forgotten by all: people whom we once knew to be very prosperous are now beneath the ground, and we trample upon their graves, and often, as we pass them, we reflect that their bodies are seething with worms—of these and many other things the soul is reminded by memory. The will inclines to love One in Whom it has seen so many acts and signs of love, some of which it would like to return. In particular, the will shows the soul how this true Lover never leaves it, but goes with it everywhere and gives it life and being. Then the understanding comes forward and makes the soul realize that, for however many years it may live, it can never hope to have a better friend, for the world is full of falsehood and these pleasures which the devil pictures to it are accompanied by trials and cares and annoyances; and tells it to be certain that outside this castle it will find neither security nor peace: let it refrain from visiting one house after another when its own house is full of good things, if it will only enjoy them. How fortunate it is to be able to find all that it needs, as it were, at home, especially when it has a Host Who will put all good things into its possession, unless, like the Prodigal Son, it desires to go astray and eat the food of the swine!

It is reflections of this kind which vanquish devils. But, oh, my God and Lord, how everything is ruined by the vain habits we fall into and the way everyone else follows them! So dead is our faith that we desire what we see more than what faith tells us about—though what we actually see is that people who pursue these visible things meet with nothing but ill fortune. All this is the work of these poisonous creatures which we have been describing. For, if a man is bitten by a viper, his whole body is poisoned and swells up; and so it is in this case, and yet we take no care of ourselves. Obviously a great deal of attention will be necessary if we are to be cured and only the great mercy of God will preserve us from death. The soul will certainly suffer great trials at this time, especially if the devil sees that its character and habits are such that it is ready to make further progress: all the powers of hell will combine to drive it back again.

Ah, my Lord! It is here that we have need of Thine aid, without which we can do nothing. Of Thy mercy, allow not this soul to be deluded and led astray when its journey is but begun. Give it light so that it may see how all its welfare consists in this and may flee from evil companionship. It is a very great thing for a person to associate with others who are walking in the right way: to mix, not only with those whom he sees in the rooms where he himself is, but with those whom he knows to have entered the rooms nearer the centre, for they will be of great help to him and he can get into such close touch with them that they will take him with them. Let him have a fixed determination not to allow himself to be beaten, for, if the devil sees that he has firmly resolved to lose his life and his peace and everything that he can offer him rather than to return to the first room, he will very soon cease troubling him. Let him play the man and not be like those who went down on their knees in order to drink when they went to battle—I forget with whom—but let him be resolute, for he is going forth to fight with all the devils and there are no better weapons than the Cross.

There is one thing so important that, although I have said it on other occasions, I will repeat it once more here: it is that at the beginning one must not think of such things as spiritual favours, for that is a very poor way of starting to build such a large and beautiful edifice. If it is begun upon sand, it will all collapse: souls which build like that will never be free from annoyances and temptations. For it is not in these *dwelling places*, but in those which are farther on, that it rains manna; once there, the soul has all that it desires, because it desires only what is the will of God. It is a curious thing: here we are, meeting with hindrances and suffering from imperfections by the thousand, with our virtues so young that they have not yet learned how to walk—in fact, they have only just been born: God grant that they have even been born at all!—and yet we are not ashamed to be wanting consolations in prayer and to be complaining about periods of aridity. This must not be true of you, sisters: embrace the Cross which your Spouse bore upon His shoulders and realize that this Cross is yours to carry too: let her who is capable of the greatest suffering suffer most for Him and she will have the most perfect freedom. All other things are of quite secondary importance: if the Lord should grant them to you, give Him heartfelt thanks.

You may think that you will be full of determination to resist outward trials if God will only grant you inward favours. His Majesty knows best what is suitable for us; it is not for us to advise Him what to give us, for He can rightly reply that we know not what we ask. All that the beginner in prayer has to do—and you must not forget this, for it is very important—is to labour and be resolute and prepare himself with all possible diligence to bring his will into conformity with the will of God. As I shall say later, you may be quite sure that this comprises the very greatest perfection which can be attained on the spiritual road. The more perfectly a person practices it, the more he will receive of the Lord and the greater the progress he will make on this road; do not think we have to use strange jargon or dabble in things of which we have no knowledge or understanding, our entire welfare is to be found in what I have described. If we go astray at the very beginning and want the Lord to do our will and to lead us just as our fancy dictates, how can this building possibly have a firm foundation? Let us see that we do as much as in us lies and avoid these venomous reptiles, for often it is the Lord's will that we should be persecuted and afflicted by evil thoughts, which we cannot cast out, and also by aridities; and sometimes He even allows these reptiles to bite us, so that we may learn better how to be on our guard in the future and see if we are really grieved at having offended Him.

If, then, you sometimes fail, do not lose heart, or cease striving to make progress, for even out of your fall God will bring good, just as a man selling an antidote will drink poison before he takes it in order to prove its power. If nothing else could show us what wretched creatures we are and what harm we do to ourselves by dissipating our desires, this war which goes on within us would be sufficient to do so and to lead us back to recollection. Can any evil be greater than the evil which we find in our own house? What hope can we have of being able to rest in other people's homes if we cannot rest in our own? For none of our friends and relatives are as near to us as our faculties, with which we have always to live, whether we like it or not, and yet our faculties seem to be making war upon us, as if they were resentful of the war made upon them by our vices. "Peace, peace," said the Lord, my sisters, and many a time He spoke words of peace to His Apostles. Believe me, unless we have peace, and strive for peace in our own home, we shall not find it in the homes of others. Let this war now cease. By the blood which Christ shed for us, I beg this of those who have not begun to enter within themselves; and those who have begun to do so must not allow such warfare to turn them back. They must realize that to fall a second time is worse than to fall once. They can see that it will lead them to ruin: let them place their trust, not in themselves, but in the mercy of God, and they will see how His Majesty can lead them on from one group of Mansions to another and set them on safe ground where these beasts cannot harass or hurt them, for He will place the beasts in their power and laugh them to scorn; and then they themselves—even in this life, I mean—will enjoy many more good things than they could ever desire.

As I said first of all, I have already written to you about how you ought to behave when you have to suffer these disturbances with which the devil torments you; and about how recollection cannot be begun by making strenuous efforts, but must come gently, after which you will be able to practice it for longer periods at a time. So I will say no more about this now, except that it is very important for you to consult people of experience; for otherwise you will imagine that you are doing yourselves great harm by pursuing your necessary occupations. But, provided we do not abandon our prayer, the Lord will turn everything we do to our profit, even though we may find no one to teach us. There is no remedy for this evil of which we have been speaking except to start again at the beginning; otherwise the soul will keep on losing a little more every day—please God that it may come to realize this.

Some of you might suppose that, if it is such a bad thing to turn back, it would have been better never to have begun, but to have remained outside the castle. I told you, however, at the outset, and the Lord Himself says this, that he who goes into danger shall perish in it, and that the door by which we can enter this castle is prayer. It is absurd to think that we can enter Heaven without first entering our own souls—without getting to know ourselves, and reflecting upon the wretchedness of our nature and what we owe to God, and continually imploring His mercy. The Lord Himself says: "No one will ascend to My Father, but by Me" (I am not sure if those are the exact words, but I think they are) and "He that sees Me sees My Father." Well, if we never look at Him or think of what we owe Him, and of the death which He suffered for our sakes, I do not see how we can get to know Him or do good works in His service. For what can be the value of faith without works, or of works which are not united with the merits of our Lord Jesus Christ? And what but such thoughts can arouse us to love this Lord? May it please His Majesty to grant us to understand how much we cost Him, that the servant is not greater than his Lord, that we must needs work if we would enjoy His glory, and that for that reason we must perforce pray, lest we enter continually into temptation.[34]

We thus end our exploration of the ways of the interior life in the shadow of the wisdom and prayers of one of the greatest masters of the spiritual life ever known to the Church. Still, this admonition may not apply to the reader and, God willing, if it does, it won't apply for very long because you will move beyond this phase at a reasonable pace. If you have discerned that you are already beyond the purgative way or are just dead serious about continuing this pursuit of God, then I strongly recommend that you continue your spiritual development through acquiring a director and reviewing the following works: *The Three Ages of the Interior Life* by Fr. Garrigou-Lagrange, and Adolf Tanquerey's *Spiritual Life*. A very engaging and accessible treatment of these phases of spiritual growth and perhaps the best available to the modern reader is Ralph Martin's book and workbook entitled *The Fulfillment of All Desire*, published by Emmaus Road Publishing. For more recommendations on the best books geared to aid you in your spiritual life, we have provided a "Resources for Growth" page at www.SpiritualDirection.com/MustRead.

DEVELOPING A RULE OF LIFE

Before we conclude this handbook, it is important to review the great benefit souls can receive by developing a "rule of life" (also referred to as a "program of life" or a "plan of life"). In religious life, a rule of life is a set of principles, prescriptions, and prohibitions that a person commits to in order to maintain a relationship with God and the community within the order. A rule of life, as applied to those of us who do not belong to a religious community, is more of a personalized creed or plan that acts as our "compass" and helps us to stay on the right path as determined through the spiritual evaluation exercises. Paragraph 88 of *The Priest, Minister of Divine Mercy* says this about developing a plan for spiritual growth:

> The journey of spiritual direction can opportunely be embarked upon by a general revision of one's life. It is always useful to have a plan or some particular resolutions covering our relationship with God (liturgical and personal prayer), our fraternal relationships, the family, work, friendships, the specific virtues, our personal duties. Such plans can also reflect our aspirations, the difficulties we encounter, and the desire to give ourselves increasingly to God. It is very useful to indicate precisely the spiritual method which one intends to adopt for the journey towards prayer, holiness (virtue), the duties of state, mortification and for the minor daily hardships of life.

As the reader likely has deduced, all of the work done this far in this book is prime material for the development of a plan for spiritual growth. A good program or rule of life will include the following elements that would reflect an emphasis or effort that could span weeks, months, or an entire year depending on whatever is necessary for effective growth:

Period of Time: What period will this rule cover (month/year)?

Root Sin Identification: What is your root sin and how does it manifest in your life?

Corresponding Virtue: What is the corresponding virtue that you will pursue that will help you fight your root sin?

Virtue in Christ: How does that virtue manifest itself in the life and person of Christ and in what way is Christ's example specifically inspiring to you in your pursuit of holiness? How will you specifically attempt to live out that virtue?

Prayer and the Sacraments: How do you plan to grow in faith through prayer and the sacraments?

Daily Schedule: How will you live your rule of life on a daily basis? This might include specific times for morning prayer, other prayer, examination of conscience, etc. This schedule might also indicate which of the scheduled items are non-negotiable commitments, and which are optional in the sense that you wouldn't violate your rule of life if you were not able to accomplish them on any particular day.

As you might suspect, a rule of life can be very detailed or very simple. From the simple end of the spectrum, a rule can simply be one sheet of paper that reflects certain types of prayer and other commitments that we might keep according to a specific schedule each day. An example of a brief focus point and a schedule might look like this:

Focus Point: This week I want to work on ensuring that I am gentle and respectful to my spouse and family—particularly when I get interrupted when I am trying to get work done. When the interruption comes, I will stop my work, turn to them, and engage with love and gentleness.

Schedule:

7:00 a.m. to 7:10 a.m.	Meditation
7:10 a.m. to 7:20 a.m.	Scripture Reading and Reflection
7:20 a.m. to 7:30 a.m.	Decade of the Rosary
11:50 a.m. to 12:00 p.m.	Angelus
12:00 p.m. to 1:00 p.m.	Mass
4:30 p.m.	Start ramping down work for the day so I can leave on time
5:00 p.m.	Leave work to get home on time for dinner with family
6:00 p.m. to 7:00 p.m.	Dinner with Family/Rosary
8:30 p.m. to 8:45 p.m.	Examination of Conscience and Night Prayer

An even simpler way to start is to write out how we might react when confronted with a frequent temptation. This approach might simply have the focus point like the one mentioned above without a schedule that might look like this:

Focus Point: Every time I have thoughts or temptation about _____, I will begin to pray the Hail Mary until they dissipate.

A key ingredient in a good rule of life is to be as specific and focused as is possible. Emphasis on everything is emphasis on nothing; it is very easy to be ambiguous or to focus on too many things at once when seeking to gain traction in the spiritual life. Guidance for being specific is similar to that provided earlier for root sin identification: If you can explain it to a stranger, then you are probably clear enough. With respect to the specific pursuit of any virtue or spiritual discipline, here's a commonly used test to determine if your spiritual goals are S.M.A.R.T:

Specific: Are my spiritual goals precise, detailed, and explicit?

Measurable: Have I stated my spiritual goals in a way that I can easily determine if I have achieved them or not?

Actionable: Are my spiritual goals clear enough that I can take daily steps toward achieving them?

Realistic: Are my spiritual goals high but within reach of someone with my responsibilities as a mother/father, wife/husband, etc.?

Time Bound: Are my goals tied to increments of time like days, weeks, months or years so that I have the added benefit of working against a specific schedule?

One note of caution: This exercise is best done with the aid of a spiritual director. At the very minimum we need the eyes of another who has gone through this process and who has a good understanding of the necessary components. Worst case, we should work on this with a spouse or a trusted spiritual friend who can provide us with objective feedback, and always with much prayer. As well, the organizations mentioned in the "shortcut" section should be familiar with the concept of having a rule of life and may be able to provide assistance. These organizations will likely have both a general rule of life that outlines the practices and commitments of members and a personal rule of life that you would develop that reflects how these elements will play out in your own life on a day-to-day basis.

Finally, regardless of the specific approach we take, at the end of each day we should do a brief examination with our night prayers to determine how we did. During this time we can review the focus points or commitments we have made, thank God for the positive progress during the day, ask forgiveness for the areas where we fail, and make note of different ways we might make more progress tomorrow.

CONCLUSION

Some time ago a man was found dead in the California desert. After an investigation the authorities determined that his car had broken down and that he had walked for miles but never made it to shelter from the heat. The incredibly sad irony is that he died just a few yards away from an aqueduct. Amazingly, he had walked for some distance on a parallel course with the abundant flow of fresh water. At first this seemed strange to the investigators, but they soon recognized that he had no way of knowing that the water was there because from where he stood, the dull amorphous terrain hid the life sustaining water and because of the smooth concrete he would not have been able to hear it. So, he died just a short distance from all the water he would have ever needed to survive.

The Church faces a similar challenge. Millions stand within just a few feet of the grace necessary to ascend to the heights of heaven in this life (with limitations, of course) and to meet the smile of God face-to-face in the next. Many of these souls attend Mass weekly, or even daily, and they are engaged in devotions like praying the Rosary, Adoration, and regular Scripture reading. The great tragedy is that so often their religious practice is limited to an external piety, and thereby practiced in ignorance of what Jesus calls us to when He says, "You, therefore, must be perfect, as your heavenly Father is perfect" (Mt. 5:48). Many go through life without seeking or knowing how to find the great grace of having a loving relationship with Christ in this life that opens the soul in ways far beyond what it could ever imagine.

The goal of this book is to help the reader to understand, even if in the smallest ways, how to get to that great stream and in so doing enter into life in the Heart of the Bearer of the water of life. In the end, this book is about acquiring self-knowledge in the context of God. With that knowledge we know where we are, we know where the life-giving water is, and we have some sense of how to get at it.

May you find all that he has for you, drink to the full, and never be thirsty again.

Feast of Our Lady of Mount Carmel, July 16, 2012

Out of his infinite glory, may he give you the power through his Spirit for your hidden self to grow strong, so that Christ may live in your hearts through faith, and then, planted in love and built on love, you will with all the saints have strength to grasp the breadth and the length, the height and the depth; until, knowing the love of Christ, which is beyond all knowledge, you are filled with the utter fullness of God. Glory be to him whose power, working in us, can do infinitely more than we can ask or imagine; glory be to him from generation to generation in the Church and in Christ Jesus forever and ever. Amen (Eph.3:16-19, NJB).

GLOSSARY OF TERMS

Unless otherwise noted, these terms are provided by *Modern Catholic Dictionary* by John A. Hardon, S.J. (Eternal Life Publications, 2000).

affective: See **prayer, affective.**

aridity: The state of a soul devoid of sensible consolation, which makes it very difficult to pray. It may be caused by something physical, such as illness, or voluntary self-indulgence, or an act of God, who is leading a person through trial to contemplation.

appetites, disordered: Inordinate and willful desires of created things or circumstances not rightly ordered to moral or spiritual good that impede union with God and darken, defile, weaken, and torment the soul (Author).

ascetical theology: The science of the saints based on a study of their lives. It is aimed to make people holy by explaining what sanctity is and how to attain it. It is the science of leading souls in the ways of Christian perfection through growth in charity and the practice of prayer leading to contemplation. It is that part of spiritual theology which concentrates on man's cooperation with grace and the need for human effort to grow in sanctity.

attachment: An emotional dependence, either of one person on another, or of a person on some real or illusory object. Attachments play an important role in spiritual development, since the first condition for progress in sanctity is some mastery over one's inordinate attachments.

confession, devotional: The practice of regular confession even when one is not aware of mortal or even venial sins. This practice includes setting and keeping a specific schedule of self-examination and confession. This may also include the confession of past mortal or venial sins even if confessed previously in specific or in general. Devotional confession can also make note of imperfections (see **imperfections**) though they are not sufficient matter for absolution. In such case, previously confessed sins, especially related to one's predominant fault, should be mentioned. Note: This practice is not recommended for those who suffer with scrupulosity (Author).

concupiscence: Insubordination of man's desires to the dictates of reason, and the propensity of human nature to sin as a result of original sin. More commonly, it refers to the spontaneous movement of the sensitive appetites toward whatever the imagination portrays as pleasant and away from whatever it portrays as painful. However, concupiscence also includes the unruly desires of the will, such as pride, ambition, and envy.

consolation: An interior movement aroused in the soul, by which it is inflamed with love of its Creator and Lord. It is likewise consolation when one sheds tears that move to the love of God, whether it is because of sorrow for sins, or because of the sufferings of Christ our Lord, or for any other reason that is immediately directed to the praise and service of God. Consolation can also be every increase of faith, hope, and love, and all interior joy that invites and attracts to what is heavenly and to the salvation of one's soul by filling it with peace and quiet in its Creator and Lord (adapted from St. Ignatius Spiritual Exercises, 316).

contemplation: See **prayer, contemplation, infused**.

detachment: In asceticism the withholding of undue affection for creatures for the sake of the Creator. When mortal sin is involved, detachment is imperative for salvation. Detachment from creatures that are an obstacle to complete service of God is a normal condition for growth in holiness.

disposition: A quality or condition of a person necessary for the performance of some action. Commonly applied to the conditions required for the valid reception or administration of the sacraments, as the state of grace is required for the sacrament of the Eucharist or sincere contrition to receive absolution in the sacrament of penance.

disordered affections: See **attachment**.

Doctor of the Church: A title given since the Middle Ages to certain saints whose writing or preaching is outstanding for guiding the faithful in all periods of the Church's history.

dryness: See **aridity**.

examen: Reflection in God's presence on one's state of soul that has some reference to a specific adopted standard of conduct—i.e., rule of life or commitments, etc. (Author).

examen, particular: Regular prayerful examination of one's conscience by concentrating on some one particular moral failing to be overcome or virtue to be exercised. Its focus is on such external manifestations of the fault or virtue as can be remembered for periodic inventory. Particular examens are changed weekly, monthly, or otherwise in order to ensure maximum attention. They are also commonly associated with some brief invocation for divine assistance, as occasions arise for avoiding a sin or acting on a virtue. And after some time another cycle may be started of the same defects that this person has to conquer or good habits he or she needs to develop.

examination of conscience: See **examen**.

formation: The act or process of developing someone in all realms of human experience but in particular those that help the human person come to better know and love God and serve others. Although human guides may assist or guide this process, we are "formed" by God, as illustrated through the imagery of the potter (God) and the clay (soul) (Author).

imperfections: Deficiencies of character that, although not as serious as mortal or venial sins, are nonetheless obstacles to attaining Christian perfection and union with God. It is important to note that the intentional omission of an obligatory good act is sinful (e.g., missing Mass on Sunday without sufficient reason). However, the failure to do a good act that is not obligatory (e.g., not going to daily Mass), whether through human frailty or the difficulty of judging its obligation, is considered a moral imperfection. While imperfections reflect deficiencies in our character, and are obstacles to Christian perfection, they are not sins and therefore are insufficient matter for absolution. However, they may be confessed in order to settle one's conscience and to grow in the spiritual life. The scrupulous would constitute an exception, and should follow the guidance of their confessor or spiritual director in such matters (Author).

infused prayer: See **prayer, contemplation, infused.**

magisterium: The Church's teaching authority, vested in the bishops, as successors of the Apostles, under the Roman Pontiff, as successor of St. Peter. Also vested in the pope, as Vicar of Christ and visible head of the Catholic Church.

movement: An ecclesial organization with canonical recognition that provides defined paths to living out baptismal commitments, discipleship, and related sanctity through a specific spiritual lens called a "charism" that is expressed by distinctive practices of life and ways of prayer (Author).

mysticism: The supernatural state of soul in which God is known in a way that no human effort or exertion could ever succeed in producing. There is an immediate, personal experience of God that is truly extraordinary, not only in intensity and degree, but in kind. It is always the result of a special, totally unmerited grace of God. Christian mysticism differs essentially from the non-Christian mysticism of the Oriental world. It always recognizes that the reality to which it penetrates simply transcends the soul and the cosmos; there is no confusion between I and thou, but always a profound humility before the infinite Majesty of God. And in Christian mysticism all union between the soul and God is a moral union of love, in doing His will even at great sacrifice to self; there is no hint of losing one's being in God or absorption of one's personality into the divine.

orthodoxy: Right belief as compared with heterodoxy or heresy.

particular examen: See **examen, particular**.

piety: The religious sensibility of a person that reflects an attitude of reverence, respect, and devotion toward God and the things of God (Author).

penance: The virtue or disposition of heart by which one repents of one's own sins and is converted to God. Also the punishment by which one atones for sins committed, either by oneself or by others. And finally the sacrament of penance, where confessed sins committed after baptism are absolved by a priest in the name of God.

prayer, contemplation, infused: An infused supernatural gift, that originates completely outside of our will or ability in God, by which a person becomes freely absorbed in God producing a real awareness, desire, and love for Him. This often gentle or delightful encounter can yield special insights into things of the spirit and results in a deeper and tangible desire to love God and neighbor in thought, word, and deed. It is important to note that infused contemplation is a state that can be prepared for, but cannot in any way be produced by the will or desire of a person through methods or ascetical practices (Author).

prayer, meditation: Reflective prayer. The form of mental prayer in which the mind, in God's presence, thinks about God and divine things. While the affections may also be active, the stress in meditation is on the role of the intellect. Hence this is also called discursive mental prayer. The objects of meditation are mainly three: mysteries of faith; a person's better knowledge of what God wants him or her to do; and the divine will, to know how God wants to be served by the one who is meditating.

prayer, affective: Often the result of discursive meditation, affective prayer occurs when the heart and mind are engaged, with and beyond the intellect, with the object of the meditation (Author).

prayer, mental: The form of prayer in which the sentiments expressed are one's own and not those of another person, and the expression of these sentiments is mainly, if not entirely, interior and not externalized (e.g., not vocalized). Mental prayer is accomplished by internal acts of the mind and affections that are a loving and discursive (reflective) consideration of religious truths or some mystery of faith. In mental prayer the three powers of the soul are engaged: the memory, which offers the mind material for meditation; the intellect, which ponders or directly perceives the meaning of some religious truth and its implications for practice; and the will, which freely expresses its sentiments of faith, trust, and love, and (as needed) makes good resolutions based on what the memory and intellect have made known to the will (adapted from Hardon by the Author).

prayer of simplicity: Meditation replaced by a purer, more intimate prayer consisting in a simple regard or loving thought on God, or on one of His attributes, or on some mystery of the Christian faith. The soul peacefully attends to the operations of the Spirit with sentiments of love without requiring the use of mental effort (adapted from Hardon).

prayer, vocal: Any form of prayer expressed audibly using pre-written formulas (e.g., Rosary, Liturgy of the Hours, etc.).

predominant fault: The defect in us that tends to prevail over the others, and thereby over our manner of feeling, judging, sympathizing, willing, and acting. This defect has in each of us an intimate relation to our individual temperament (see Lagrange, *Three Ages,* Part 2, Chapter 22).

purification, active: This purification comes about as a result of the efforts of the soul (aided by the Holy Spirit) who seeks to purify itself from sins, vices, imperfections, and anything that would keep it from attaining holiness, union with God, and living a life that honors God and neighbor (Author).

purification, passive: This purification shares the same end as Active Purification whose means are solely of God and from God. This purification is the preparation for the exceptional graces of the supernatural life (Author).

program of life: See **rule of life**.

recollection: Concentration of soul on the presence of God.

renunciation: To give up something to which a person has a claim. Some renunciations are necessary by divine law; others are permitted and encouraged according to divine counsel. Everyone must renounce sin and those creatures that are proximate occasions to sin. In this category belongs the renunciation of Satan at Baptism, either by the person being baptized or by the sponsor. Renunciations of counsel pertain to the exercise of such natural rights as material possessions, marriage, and legitimate autonomy or self-determination, sacrificed for love of God by those who vow themselves to poverty, chastity, and obedience.

reparation: The act or fact of making amends. It implies an attempt to restore things to their normal or sound conditions, as they were before something wrong was done. It applies mainly to recompense for the losses sustained or the harm caused by some morally bad action. With respect to God, it means making up with greater love for the failure in love through sin; it means restoring what was unjustly taken and compensating with generosity for the selfishness that caused the jury.

rule of life: A specific and usually documented plan for living in accord with one's state in life and baptismal commitments that includes principals, guidelines, and commitments that will guide each person to achieve sanctity, and in practical and concrete ways, love God and love their neighbor (Author). A principle or regular mode of action, prescribed by one in authority, for the well-being of those who are members of a society. In this sense the organized methods of living the evangelical counsels are called "rules," as the Rule of St. Augustine or the Rule of St. Benedict. A rule may also be a customary standard that is not necessarily prescribed by authority, but voluntarily undertaken in order to regulate one's conduct for more effective moral living or more effective service of others.

root sin: See **predominant fault.**

scrupulosity: The habit of imagining sin where none exists, or grave sin where the matter is venial. To overcome scrupulosity, a person needs to be properly instructed in order to form a right conscience, and in extreme cases the only remedy is absolute obedience (for a time) to a prudent confessor.

self-knowledge: Personal awareness of both the dignity of the human soul and its exalted destiny, as well as knowledge of the wounds and darkness that original and personal sin has inflicted on it. This awareness is not one that is isolated to the natural order but that frames self-understanding in the context of God's presence and God's law (Author).

self-denial: The act or practice of giving up some legitimate satisfaction for the sake of some higher motive.

self-renunciation: See **renunciation.**

self-annihilation: Heroic renunciation and self-giving. See **renunciation.**

sin, mortal: An actual sin that destroys sanctifying grace and causes the supernatural death of the soul. Mortal sin is a turning away from God because of a seriously inordinate adherence to creatures that causes grave injury to a person's rational nature and to the social order, and deprives the sinner of a right to heaven.

The terms mortal, deadly, grave, and serious applied to sin are synonyms, each with a slightly different implication. Mortal and deadly focus on the effects in the sinner, namely deprivation of the state of friendship with God; grave and serious refer to the importance of the matter in which a person offends God. But the Church never distinguishes among these terms as though they represented different kinds of sins. There is only one recognized correlative to mortal sin, and that is venial sin, which offends against God but does not cause the loss of one's state of grace.

sin, near occasion of: Any person, place, or thing that of its nature or because of human frailty can lead one to do wrong, thereby committing sin. If the danger is certain and probable, the occasion is proximate; if the danger is slight, the occasion becomes remote. It is voluntary if it can easily be avoided. There is no obligation to avoid a remote occasion unless there is probable danger of its becoming proximate. There is a positive obligation to avoid a voluntary proximate occasion of sin even though the occasion of evildoing is due only to human weakness.

sin, root sin (predominant fault): The defect within us that tends to be more prominent than all the others, and thereby has the greatest influence on our manner of feeling, judging, sympathizing, willing, and acting. This defect has in each of us an intimate relation to our individual temperament (LaGrange).

sin, venial: An offense against God which does not deprive the sinner of sanctifying grace. It is called venial (from *venia pardon*) because the soul still has the vital principle that allows a cure from within, similar to the healing of a sick or diseased body whose source of animation (the soul) is still present to restore the ailing bodily function to health.

Deliberate venial sin is a disease that slackens the spiritual powers, lowers one's resistance to evil, and causes one to deviate from the path that leads to heavenly glory. Variously called "daily sins" or "light sins" or "lesser sins," they are committed under a variety of conditions: when a person transgresses with full or partial knowledge and consent to a divine law that does not oblige seriously; when one violates a law that obliges gravely but either one's knowledge or consent is not complete; or when one disobeys what is an objectively grave precept but due to invincible ignorance a person thinks the obligation is not serious.

The essence of venial sin consists in a certain disorder but does not imply complete aversion from humanity's final destiny. It is an illness of the soul rather than its supernatural death. When people commit a venial sin, they do not decisively set themselves on turning away from God, but from over-fondness for some created good fall short of God. They are like persons who loiter without leaving the way.

spiritual exercises: Any set program of religious duties, notably the prayers, meditations, and spiritual reading required of persons following a distinctive rule of life. Also the period of silence and prayerful reflection practiced annually (or more often) in a retreat. Particularly the spiritual exercises by St. Ignatius Loyola, drawn up as a method of arriving at the amendment of one's life and resolving on a determined way of holiness. The exercises of St. Ignatius were first composed by him in a cave at Manresa, in Spain, after his conversion. They have been recommended by successive popes as a most effective program of spiritual renewal for priests, religious, and the laity. Their underlying principle is their opening statement that "Man was created to praise, reverence and serve our Creator and Lord, and by this means to save his soul." Given this basic purpose of human existence, the believer is told how to reach his or her destiny by overcoming sinful tendencies and imitating Christ in carrying the Cross on earth in order to be glorified with Christ in the life to come.

spiritual marriage: See **transforming union.**

spiritual warfare: A form of prayer and personal vigilance, with humble reliance on the grace and power of God, that sets itself specifically and actively against particular forces of evil as they manifest themselves in the flesh and the world (Author).

transforming union: The highest degree of perfection attained in this life marked by a total transformation of the soul into the Beloved wherein God and the soul give themselves to each other in the ultimate consummation of divine love (Author; adapted from *Spiritual Theology*, page 350–351, Aumann, Continuum, NY, 2006).

third order: Associations of the faithful established by religious orders. Dating from the thirteenth century, they may be either secular or regular. If secular, they are laypersons, commonly called tertiaries. If regular, they are religious, bound by public vows and live in community. Originally, third orders were Franciscan or Dominican, but the Holy See has since approved many others, both secular and regular—e.g., the Augustinians, Carmelites, Servites, and Trinitarians.

APPENDIX ONE

SCHOOLS OF SPIRITUAL DIRECTION

Catholic Spiritual Mentorship Program (Apostles of the Interior Life with the School of Faith, Diocese of Kansas City, Kansas)

"In collaboration with Holy Family School of Faith, the Apostles of the Interior Life Spiritual Mentorship Program is a two-year course of study combining eight distance learning courses with four one-week intensive sessions offered in-residence at Savior Pastoral Center in Kansas City, Kansas. The program aims to form Spiritual Mentors to serve as guide and companion to others on their journey to holiness. It is designed for Catholics who have a desire to develop a deep prayer and sacramental life, a desire to increase their knowledge of the Catholic faith, a desire to grow in the virtues and a desire to help others do the same." www.SchoolOfFaith.com

Spiritual Direction Program (Marian Servants of Divine Providence, Clearwater, Florida)

"The Cenacle of Our Lady of Divine Providence® School of Spirituality has established its Spiritual Direction Program in response to Christ's call to personal holiness and the Church's need for well-trained spiritual directors to assist God's people on their spiritual journey. As a recognized institution of God's vineyard approved by the Bishop of the Diocese of St. Petersburg, Florida, and in association with the Franciscan University of Steubenville, Ohio, this program is designed to form and train candidates over a two year period through prayer, teachings and supervision. The program exposes the student to the spiritual heritage of the Church and highlights the spirituality of St. Francis of Assisi and St. Ignatius of Loyola." www.DivineProvidence.org

Spiritual Direction Training Program (Lanteri Center for Ignatian Spirituality, Denver, Colorado)

"The Lanteri Center, established by the Oblates of the Virgin Mary in 2004, exists to make spiritual direction, daily prayer with Scripture, and the spiritual exercises of St. Ignatius more available to those who seek holiness. The Lanteri Center also provides training and continuing education opportunities for spiritual directors." www.LanteriCenter.org

APPENDIX TWO

LETTER TO THE BISHOPS OF THE CATHOLIC CHURCH
ON SOME ASPECTS OF CHRISTIAN MEDITATION

Congregation for the Doctrine of the Faith, October 15, 1989

I. Introduction

1. Many Christians today have a keen desire to learn how to experience a deeper and authentic prayer life despite the not inconsiderable difficulties which modern culture places in the way of the need for silence, recollection and meditation. The interest which in recent years has been awakened also among some Christians by forms of meditation associated with some eastern religions and their particular methods of prayer is a significant sign of this need for spiritual recollection and a deep contact with the divine mystery. Nevertheless, faced with this phenomenon, many feel the need for sure criteria of a doctrinal and pastoral character which might allow them to instruct others in prayer, in its numerous manifestations, while remaining faithful to the truth revealed in Jesus, by means of the genuine Tradition of the Church. This present letter seeks to reply to this urgent need, so that in the various particular Churches the many different forms of prayer, including new ones, may never lose their correct personal and communitarian nature.

These indications are addressed in the first place to the Bishops, to be considered in that spirit of pastoral solicitude for the Churches entrusted to them, so that the entire people of God—priests, religious and laity—may again be called to pray, with renewed vigor, to the Father through the Spirit of Christ our Lord.

2. The ever more frequent contact with other religions and with their different styles and methods of prayer has, in recent decades, led many of the faithful to ask themselves what value non-Christian forms of meditation might have for Christians. Above all, the question concerns eastern methods.[1] Some people today turn to these methods for therapeutic reasons. The spiritual restlessness arising from a life subjected to the driving pace of a technologically advanced society also brings a certain number of Christians to seek in these methods of prayer a path to interior peace and psychic balance. This psychological aspect is not dealt with in the present letter, which instead emphasizes the theological and spiritual implications of the question. Other Christians, caught up in the movement towards openness and exchanges between various religions and cultures, are of the opinion that their prayer has much to gain from these methods. Observing that in recent times many traditional methods of meditation, especially Christian ones, have fallen into disuse, they wonder whether it might not now be possible, by a new training in prayer, to enrich our heritage by incorporating what has until now been foreign to it.

3. To answer this question one must first of all consider, even if only in a general way, in what does the intimate nature of Christian prayer consist. Then one can see if and how it might be enriched by meditation methods which have been developed in other religions and cultures. However, in order to achieve this, one needs to start with a certain clear premise. Christian prayer is always determined by the structure of the Christian faith, in which the very truth of God and creature shines forth. For this reason, it is defined, properly speaking, as a personal, intimate and profound dialogue between man and God. It expresses therefore the communion of redeemed creatures

with the intimate life of the Persons of the Trinity. This communion, based on Baptism and the Eucharist, source and summit of the life of the Church, implies an attitude of conversion, a flight from "self" to the "You" of God. Thus Christian prayer is at the same time always authentically personal and communitarian. It flees from impersonal techniques or from concentrating on oneself, which can create a kind of rut, imprisoning the person praying in a spiritual privatism which is incapable of a free openness to the transcendental God. Within the Church, in the legitimate search for new methods of meditation it must always be borne in mind that the essential element of authentic Christian prayer is the meeting of two freedoms, the infinite freedom of God with the finite freedom of man.

II. Christian Prayer in the Light of Revelation

4. The Bible itself teaches how the man who welcomes biblical revelation should pray. In the Old Testament there is a marvelous collection of prayers which have continued to live through the centuries, even within the Church of Jesus Christ, where they have become the basis of its official prayer: The Book of Praises or of Psalms.[2] Prayers similar to the Psalms may also be found in earlier Old Testament texts or re-echoed in later ones.[3] The prayers of the book of Psalms tell in the first place of God's great works on behalf of the Chosen People. Israel meditates, contemplates and makes the marvels of God present again, recalling them in prayer. In biblical revelation Israel came to acknowledge and praise God present in all creation and in the destiny of every man. Thus he is invoked, for example, as rescuer in time of danger, in sickness, in persecution, in tribulation. Finally, and always in the light of his salvific works, he is exalted in his divine power and goodness, in his justice and mercy, in his royal grandeur.

5. Thanks to the words, deeds, passion and resurrection of Jesus Christ, in the "New Testament" the faith acknowledges in him the definitive self-revelation of God, the Incarnate Word who reveals the most inti-

mate depth of his love. It is the Holy Spirit, he who was sent into the hearts of the faithful, he who "searches everything, even the depths of God" (1 Cor. 2:10), who makes it possible to enter into these divine depths. According to the promise Jesus made to the disciples, the Spirit will explain all that he had not yet been able to tell them. However, this Spirit "will not speak on his own authority," but "he will glorify me, for he will take what is mine and declare it to you" (Jn. 16:13f.). What Jesus calls "his" is, as he explains immediately, also God the Father's because "all that the Father has is mine; therefore I said that he will take what is mine and declare it to you" (Jn. 16:15).

The authors of the New Testament, with full cognizance, always spoke of the revelation of God in Christ within the context of a vision illuminated by the Holy Spirit. The Synoptic Gospels narrate Jesus' deeds and words on the basis of a deeper understanding, acquired after Easter, of what the disciples had seen and heard. The entire Gospel of St. John is taken up with the contemplation of him who from the beginning is the Word of God made flesh. Paul, to whom Jesus appeared in his divine majesty on the road to Damascus, instructs the faithful so that they "may have power to comprehend with all the saints what is the breadth and length and height and depth [of the mystery of Christ], and to know the love of Christ which surpasses all knowledge, that you may be filled with all the fullness of God" (Eph 3:18 ff.). For Paul the mystery of God is Christ, "in whom are hidden all the treasures of wisdom and knowledge" (Col 2:3) and, the Apostle clarifies, "I say this in order that no one may delude you with beguiling speech" (v. 4).

6. There exists, then, a strict relationship between revelation and prayer. The Dogmatic Constitution "Dei Verbum" teaches that by means of his revelation the invisible God, "from the fullness of his love, addresses men as his friends (cf. Ex 33:11; Jn. 15:14–15), and moves among them (cf. Bar 3:38), in order to invite and receive them into his own company."[4] This revelation takes place through words

and actions which have a constant mutual reference, one to the other; from the beginning everything proceeds to converge on Christ, the fullness of revelation and of grace, and on the gift of the Holy Spirit. These make man capable of welcoming and contemplating the words and works of God and of thanking him and adoring him, both in the assembly of the faithful and in the intimacy of his own heart illuminated by grace.

This is why the Church recommends the reading of the Word of God as a source of Christian prayer, and at the same time exhorts all to discover the deep meaning of Sacred Scripture through prayer "so that a dialogue takes place between God and man. For, 'we speak to him when we pray; we listen to him when we read the divine oracles.'"[5]

7. Some consequences derive immediately from what has been called to mind. If the prayer of a Christian has to be inserted in the Trinitarian movement of God, then its essential content must also necessarily be determined by the twofold direction of such movement. It is in the Holy Spirit that the Son comes into the world to reconcile it to the Father through his works and sufferings. On the other hand, in this same movement and in the very same Spirit, the Son Incarnate returns to the Father, fulfilling his will through his passion and resurrection. The "Our Father," Jesus' own prayer, clearly indicates the unity of this movement: the will of the Father must be done on earth as it is in heaven (the petitions for bread, forgiveness and protection make explicit the fundamental dimensions of God's will for us), so that there may be a new earth in the heavenly Jerusalem.

The prayer of Jesus[6] has been entrusted to the Church ("Pray then like this"—Lk. 11:2). This is why when a Christian prays, even if he is alone, his prayer is in fact always within the framework of the "communion of saints" in which and with which he prays, whether in a public and liturgical way or in a private manner. Consequently, it must always be offered within the authentic spirit of the Church at prayer, and therefore under its guidance, which can sometimes take a concrete form in terms of a proven spiritual direction. The Christian, even when he is alone and prays in secret, is conscious that he always prays for the good of the Church in union with Christ, in the Holy Spirit and together with all the saints.[7]

III. Erroneous Ways of Praying

8. Even in the first centuries of the Church some incorrect forms of prayer crept in. Some New Testament texts (cf. 1 Jn. 4:3; 1 Tim 1:3–7 and 4:3–4) already give hints of their existence. Subsequently, two fundamental deviations came to be identified: Pseudognosticism and Messalianism, both of concern to the Fathers of the Church. There is much to be learned from that experience of primitive Christianity and the reaction of the Fathers which can help in tackling the current problem.

In combating the errors of "pseudognosticism"[8] the Fathers affirmed that matter is created by God and as such is not evil. Moreover, they maintained that grace, which always has the Holy Spirit as its source is not a good proper to the soul, but must be sought from God as a gift. Consequently, the illumination or superior knowledge of the Spirit ("gnosis") does not make Christian faith something superfluous. Finally, for the Fathers, the authentic sign of a superior knowledge, the fruit of prayer, is always Christian love.

9. If the perfection of Christian prayer cannot be evaluated using the sublimity of nostic knowledge as a basis, neither can it be judged by referring to the experience of the divine, as "Messalianism" proposed.[9] These false fourth-century charismatics identified the grace of the Holy Spirit with the psychological experience of his presence in the soul. In opposing them, the Fathers insisted on the fact that the soul's union with God in prayer is realized in a mysterious way, and in particular through the sacraments of the Church. Moreover, it can even be achieved through experiences of affliction or desolation. Contrary to the view of the Mes-

salians, these are not necessarily a sign that the Spirit has abandoned a soul. Rather, as masters of spirituality have always clearly acknowledged, they may be an authentic participation in the state of abandonment experienced on the cross by our Lord, who always remains the model and mediator of prayer.[10]

10. Both of these forms of error continue to be a "temptation for man the sinner." They incite him to try and overcome the distance separating creature from Creator, as though there ought not to be such a distance; to consider the way of Christ on earth, by which he wishes to lead us to the Father, as something now surpassed; to bring down to the level of natural psychology what has been regarded as pure grace, considering it instead as "superior knowledge" or as "experience."

Such erroneous forms, having reappeared in history from time to time on the fringes of the Church's prayer, seem once more to impress many Christians, appealing to them as a kind of remedy, be it psychological or spiritual, or as a quick way of finding God.[11]

11. However, these forms of error, wherever they arise, "can be diagnosed" very simply. The meditation of the Christian in prayer seeks to grasp the depths of the divine in the salvific works of God in Christ, the Incarnate Word, and in the gift of his Spirit. These divine depths are always revealed to him through the human-earthly dimension. Similar methods of meditation, on the other hand, including those which have their starting-point in the words and deeds of Jesus, try as far as possible to put aside everything that is worldly, sense perceptible or conceptually limited. It is thus an attempt to ascend to or immerse oneself in the sphere of the divine, which, as such, is neither terrestrial, sense-perceptible nor capable of conceptualization.[12] This tendency, already present in the religious sentiments of the later Greek period (especially in "Neoplatonism"), is found deep in the religious inspiration of many peoples, no sooner than they become aware of the

precarious character of their representations of the divine and of their attempts to draw close to it.

12. With the present diffusion of eastern methods of meditation in the Christian world and in ecclesial communities, we find ourselves faced with a pointed renewal of an attempt, which is not free from dangers and errors, "to fuse Christian meditation with that which is non-Christian." Proposals in this direction are numerous and radical to a greater or lesser extent. Some use eastern methods solely as a psycho-physical preparation for a truly Christian contemplation; others go further and, using different techniques, try to generate spiritual experiences similar to those described in the writings of certain Catholic mystics.[13] Still others do not hesitate to place that absolute without image or concepts, which is proper to Buddhist theory,[14] on the same level as the majesty of God revealed in Christ, which towers above finite reality. To this end, they make use of a "negative theology," which transcends every affirmation seeking to express what God is, and denies that the things of this world can offer traces of the infinity of God. Thus they propose abandoning not only meditation on the salvific works accomplished in history by the God of the Old and New Covenant, but also the very idea of the One and Triune God, who is Love, in favor of an immersion "in the indeterminate abyss of the divinity."[15] These and similar proposals to harmonize Christian meditation with eastern techniques need to have their contents and methods ever subjected to a thorough-going examination so as to avoid the danger of falling into syncretism.

IV. The Christian Way to Union With God

13. To find the right "way" of prayer, the Christian should consider what has been said earlier regarding the prominent features of the "way of Christ," whose "food is to do the will of him who sent [him], and to accomplish his work" (Jn. 4:34). Jesus lives no more intimate or closer a union with the Father than this, which for him is continually translated

into deep prayer. By the will of the Father he is sent to mankind, to sinners, to his very executioners, and he could not be more intimately united to the Father than by obeying his will. This did not in any way prevent him, however, from also retiring to a solitary place during his earthly sojourn to unite himself to the Father and receive from him new strength for his mission in this world. On Mount Tabor, where his union with the Father was manifest, there was called to mind his passion (cf. Lk. 9:31), and there was not even a consideration of the possibility of remaining in "three booths" on the Mount of the Transfiguration. Contemplative Christian prayer always leads to love of neighbor, to action and to the acceptance of trials, and precisely because of this it draws one close to God.

14. In order to draw near to that mystery of union with God, which the Greek Fathers called the "divinization" of man, and to grasp accurately the manner in which this is realized, it is necessary in the first place to bear in mind that man is essentially a creature,[16] and remains such for eternity, so that an absorbing of the human self into the divine self is never possible, not even in the highest states of grace. However, one must recognize that the human person is created in the "image and likeness" of God, and that the archetype of this image is the Son of God, in whom and through whom we have been created (cf. Col 1:16). This archetype reveals the greatest and most beautiful Christian mystery: from eternity the Son is "other" with respect to the Father and yet, in the Holy Spirit, he is "of the same substance." Consequently this otherness, far from being an ill, is rather the greatest of goods. There is otherness in God himself, who is one single nature in three Persons, and there is also otherness between God and creatures, who are by nature different. Finally, in the Holy Eucharist, as in the rest of the sacraments—and analogically in his works and in his words—Christ gives himself to us and makes us participate in his divine nature,[17] without nevertheless suppressing our created nature, in which he himself shares through his Incarnation.

15. A consideration of these truths together brings the wonderful discovery that all the aspirations which the prayer of other religions expresses are fulfilled in the reality of Christianity beyond all measure, without the personal self or the nature of a creature being dissolved or disappearing into the sea of the Absolute. "God is love" (1 Jn. 4:8). This profoundly Christian affirmation can reconcile perfect "union" with the "otherness" existing between lover and loved, with eternal exchange and eternal dialogue. God is himself this eternal exchange and we can truly become sharers of Christ, as "adoptive sons" who cry out with the Son in the Holy Spirit, Abba, Father." In this sense, the Fathers are perfectly correct in speaking of the divinization of man who, having been incorporated into Christ, the Son of God by nature, may by his grace share in the divine nature and become a "son in the Son." Receiving the Holy Spirit, the Christian glorifies the Father and really shares in the Trinitarian life of God.

V. Questions of Method

16. The majority of the "great religions" which have sought union with God in prayer have also pointed out ways to achieve it. Just as "the Catholic Church rejects nothing of what is true and holy in these religions,"[18] neither should these ways be rejected out of hand simply because they are not Christian. On the contrary, one can take from them what is useful so long as the Christian conception of prayer, its logic and requirements are never obscured. It is within the context of all of this that these bits and pieces should be taken up and expressed anew. Among these one might mention first of all that of the humble acceptance of a master who is an expert in the life of prayer, and of the counsels he gives. Christian experience has known of this practice from earliest times, from the epoch of the desert Fathers. Such a master, being an expert in "sentire cum ecclesia," must not only direct and warn of certain dangers; as a "spiritual father," he has to also lead his pupil in a dynamic way, heart to heart, into the life of prayer, which is the gift of the Holy Spirit.

17. In the later non-Christian classical period, there was a convenient distinction made between three stages in the life of perfection: the purgative way, the illuminative way and the unitive way. This teaching has served as a model for many schools of Christian spirituality. While in itself valid, this analysis nevertheless requires several clarifications so as to be interpreted in a correct Christian manner which avoids dangerous misunderstandings.

18. The seeking of God through prayer has to be preceded and accompanied by an ascetical struggle and a purification from one's own sins and errors, since Jesus has said that only "the pure of heart shall see God" (Mt 5:8). The Gospel aims above all at a moral purification from the lack of truth and love and, on a deeper level, from all the selfish instincts which impede man from recognizing and accepting the will of God in its purity. The passions are not negative in themselves (as the Stoics and Neoplatonists thought), but their tendency is to selfishness. It is from this that the Christian has to free himself in order to arrive at that state of positive freedom which in classical Christian times was called "apatheia," in the Middle Ages "Impassibilitas" and in the Ignatian Spiritual Exercises "indiferencia."[19]

This is impossible without a radical self-denial, as can also be seen in St. Paul who openly uses the word "mortification" (of sinful tendencies).[20] Only this self-denial renders man free to carry out the will of God and to share in the freedom of the Holy Spirit.

19. Therefore, one has to interpret correctly the teaching of those masters who recommend "emptying" the spirit of all sensible representations and of every concept, while remaining lovingly attentive to God. In this way, the person praying creates an empty space which can then be filled by the richness of God. However, the emptiness which God requires is that of the renunciation of personal selfishness, not necessarily that of the renunciation of those created things which he has given us and among which

he has placed us. There is no doubt that in prayer one should concentrate entirely on God and as far as possible exclude the things of this world which bind us to our selfishness. On this topic St. Augustine is an excellent teacher: if you want to find God, he says, abandon the exterior world and re-enter into yourself. However, he continues, do not remain in yourself, but go beyond yourself because you are not God; he is deeper and greater than you. "I look for his substance in my soul and I do not find it; I have however meditated on the search for God and, reaching out to him, through created things, I have sought to know 'the invisible perfections of God' (Rom 1:20)."[21] "To remain in oneself": this is the real danger. The great Doctor of the Church recommends concentrating on oneself, but also transcending the self which is not God, but only a creature. God is "deeper than my inmost being and higher than my greatest height."[22] In fact God is in us and with us, but he transcends us in his mystery.[23]

20. "From the dogmatic point of view," it is impossible to arrive at a perfect love of God if one ignores his giving of himself to us through his Incarnate Son, who was crucified and rose from the dead. In him, under the action of the Holy Spirit, we participate, through pure grace, in the interior life of God. When Jesus says, "He who has seen me has seen the Father" (Jn. 14:9), he does not mean just the sight and exterior knowledge of his human figure (in the flesh is of no avail"—Jn. 6:63). What he means is rather a vision made possible by the grace of faith: to see, through the manifestation of Jesus perceptible by the senses, just what he, as the Word of the Father, truly wants to reveal to us of God ("It is the Spirit that gives life [...]; the words that I have spoken to you are spirit and life"—ibid.). This "seeing" is not a matter of a purely human abstraction ("abstractio") from the figure in which God has revealed himself; it is rather the grasping of the divine reality in the human figure of Jesus, his eternal divine dimension in its temporal form. As St. Ignatius says in the "Spiritual Exercises," we should try to capture "the infinite perfume and the infinite sweetness of the divinity" (n. 124), going forward from that

finite revealed truth from which we have begun. While he raises us up, God is free to "empty" us of all that holds us back in this world, to draw us completely into the Trinitarian life of his eternal love. However, this gift can only be granted "in Christ through the Holy Spirit," and not through our own efforts, withdrawing ourselves from his revelation.

21. On the path of the Christian life, illumination follows on from purification, through the love which the Father bestows on us in the Son and the anointing which we receive from him in the Holy Spirit (cf. 1 Jn. 2:20). Ever since the early Christian period, writers have referred to the "illumination" received in Baptism. After their initiation into the divine mysteries, this illumination brings the faithful to know Christ by means of the faith which works through love. Some ecclesiastical writers even speak explicitly of the illumination received in Baptism as the basis of that sublime knowledge of Christ Jesus (cf. Phil 3:8), which is defined as "theoria" or contemplation.[24] The faithful, with the grace of Baptism, are called to progress in the knowledge and witness of the mysteries of the faith by "the intimate sense of spiritual realities which they experience."[25] No light from God can render the truths of the faith redundant. Any subsequent graces of illumination which God may grant rather help to make clearer the depth of the mysteries confessed and celebrated by the Church, as we wait for the day when the Christian can contemplate God as he is in glory (cf. 1 Jn. 3:2).

22. Finally, the Christian who prays can, if God so wishes, come to a particular experience of "union." The Sacraments, especially Baptism and the Eucharist,[26] are the objective beginning of the union of the Christian with God. Upon this foundation, the person who prays can be called, by a special grace of the Spirit, to that specific type of union with God which in Christian terms is called "mystical."

23. Without doubt, a Christian needs certain periods of retreat into solitude to be recollected and, in God's presence, rediscover his path. Never-

theless, given his character as a creature, and as a creature who knows that only in grace is he secure, his method of getting closer to God is not based on any "technique" in the strict sense of the word. That would contradict the spirit of childhood called for by the Gospel. Genuine Christian mysticism has nothing to do with technique: it is always a gift of God, and the one who benefits from it knows himself to be unworthy.[27]

24. There are certain "mystical graces," conferred on the founders of ecclesial institutes to benefit their foundation, and on other saints, too, which characterize their personal experience of prayer and which cannot, as such, be the object of imitation and aspiration for other members of the faithful, even those who belong to the same institutes and those who seek an ever more perfect way of prayer.[28] There can be different levels and different ways of sharing in a founder's experience of prayer, without everything having to be exactly the same. Besides, the prayer experience that is given a privileged position in all genuinely ecclesial institutes, ancient and modern, is always in the last analysis something personal. And it is to the individual person that God gives his graces for prayer.

25. With regard to mysticism, one has to distinguish between "the gifts of the Holy Spirit and the charisms" granted by God in a totally gratuitous way. The former are something which every Christian can quicken in himself by his zeal for the life of faith, hope and charity; and thus, by means of a serious ascetical struggle, he can reach a certain experience of God and of the contents of the faith. As for charisms, St. Paul says that these are, above all, for the benefit of the Church, of the other members of the Mystical Body of Christ (cf. 1 Cor. 12:17). With this in mind, it should be remembered that charisms are not the same things as extraordinary ("mystical") gifts (cf. Rom 12:3–21), and that the distinction between the "gifts of the Holy Spirit" and "charisms" can be flexible. It is certain that a charism which bears fruit for the Church, cannot, in the context of the New Testament, be exercised without a certain degree of personal perfection, and that, on the other hand, every "living" Chris-

tian has a specific task (and in this sense a "charism") "for the building up of the body of Christ" (cf. Eph 4:15–16),[29] in communion with the hierarchy whose job it is "not indeed to extinguish the Spirit, but to test all things and hold fast to what is good" (LG, n. 12).

VI. Psychological-Corporal Methods

26. Human experience shows that the "position and demeanor of the body" also have their influence on the recollection and dispositions of the spirit. This is a fact to which some eastern and western Christian spiritual writers have directed their attention.

Their reflections, while presenting points in common with eastern non-Christian methods of meditation, avoid the exaggerations and partiality of the latter, which, however, are often recommended to people today who are not sufficiently prepared.

The spiritual authors have adopted those elements which make recollection in prayer easier, at the same time recognizing their relative value: they are useful if reformulated in accordance with the aim of Christian prayer.[30] For example, the Christian fast signifies, above all, an exercise of penitence and sacrifice; but, already for the Fathers, it also had the aim of rendering man more open to the encounter with God and making a Christian more capable of self-dominion and at the same time more attentive to those in need.

In prayer it is the whole man who must enter into relation with God, and so his body should also take up the position most suited to recollection.[31] Such a position can in a symbolic way express the prayer itself, depending on cultures and personal sensibilities. In some aspects, Christians are today becoming more conscious of how one's bodily posture can aid prayer.

27. Eastern Christian meditation[32] has valued "psychophysical symbolism," often absent in western forms of prayer. It can range from a spe-

cific bodily posture to the basic life functions, such as breathing or the beating of the heart. The exercise of the "Jesus Prayer," for example, which adapts itself to the natural rhythm of breathing can, at least for a certain time, be of real help to many people.[33] On the other hand, the eastern masters themselves have also noted that not everyone is equally suited to making use of this symbolism, since not everybody is able to pass from the material sign to the spiritual reality that is being sought.

Understood in an inadequate and incorrect way, the symbolism can even become an idol and thus an obstacle to the raising up of the spirit to God. To live out in one's prayer the full awareness of one's body as a symbol is even more difficult: it can degenerate into a cult of the body and can lead surreptitiously to considering all bodily sensations as spiritual experiences.

28. Some physical exercises automatically produce a feeling of quiet and relaxation, pleasing sensations, perhaps even phenomena of light and of warmth, which resemble spiritual well-being. To take such feelings for the authentic consolations of the Holy Spirit would be a totally erroneous way of conceiving the spiritual life. Giving them a symbolic significance typical of the mystical experience, when the moral condition of the person concerned does not correspond to such an experience, would represent a kind of mental schizophrenia which could also lead to psychic disturbance and, at times, to moral deviations.

That does not mean that genuine practices of meditation which come from the Christian East and from the great non-Christian religions, which prove attractive to the man of today who is divided and disoriented, cannot constitute a suitable means of helping the person who prays to come before God with an interior peace, even in the midst of external pressures.

It should, however, be remembered that habitual union with God, namely that attitude of interior vigilance and appeal to the divine assistance which in the New Testament is called "continuous prayer,"[34] is not necessarily interrupted when one devotes oneself also, according to the will of God, to work and to the care of one's neighbor. "So, whether you eat or drink, or whatever you do, do all to the glory of God," the Apostle tells us (1 Cor. 10:31). In fact, genuine prayer, as the great spiritual masters teach, stirs up in the person who prays an ardent charity which moves him to collaborate in the mission of the Church and to serve his brothers for the greater glory of God.[35]

VII. "I Am The Way"

29. From the rich variety of Christian prayer as proposed by the Church, each member of the faithful should seek and find his own way, his own form of prayer. But all of these personal ways, in the end, flow into the way to the Father, which is how Jesus Christ has described himself. In the search for his own way, each person will, therefore, let himself be led not so much by his personal tastes as by the Holy Spirit, who guides him, through Christ, to the Father.

30. For the person who makes a serious effort there will, however, be moments in which he seems to be wandering in a desert and, in spite of all his efforts, he "feels" nothing of God. He should know that these trials are not spared anyone who takes prayer seriously. However, he should not immediately see this experience, common to all Christians who pray, as the "dark night" in the mystical sense. In any case in these moments, his prayer, which he will resolutely strive to keep to, could give him the impression of a certain "artificiality," although really it is something totally different: in fact it is at that very moment an expression of his fidelity to God, in whose presence he wishes to remain even when he receives no subjective consolation in return.

In these apparently negative moments, it becomes clear what the person who is praying really seeks: is he indeed looking for God who, in his infinite freedom, always surpasses him; or is he only seeking himself, without managing to go beyond his own "experiences," whether they be positive "experiences" of union with God or negative "experiences" of mystical "emptiness."

31. The love of God, the sole object of Christian contemplation, is a reality which cannot be "mastered" by any method or technique. On the contrary, we must always have our sights fixed on Jesus Christ, in whom God's love went to the cross for us and there assumed even the condition of estrangement from the Father (cf. Mk 13:34). We therefore should allow God to decide the way he wishes to have us participate in his love. But we can never, in any way, seek to place ourselves on the same level as the object of our contemplation. the free love of God; not even when, through the mercy of God the Father and the Holy Spirit sent into our hearts, we receive in Christ the gracious gift of a sensible reflection of that divine love and we feel drawn by the truth and beauty and goodness of the Lord.

The more a creature is permitted to draw near to God, the greater his reverence before the thrice-holy God. One then understands those words of St. Augustine: "You can call me friend; I recognize myself a servant."[36] Or the words which are even more familiar to us, spoken by her who was rewarded with the highest degree of intimacy with God: "He has looked upon his servant in her lowliness" (Lk. 1:48).

The Supreme Pontiff, John Paul II, in an audience granted to the under-signed Cardinal Prefect, gave his approval to this letter, drawn up in a plenary session of this Congregation, and ordered its publication.

At Rome, from the offices of the Congregation for the Doctrine of the Faith, October 15, 1989, the Feast of Saint Teresa of Jesus.

Joseph Card. Ratzinger Prefect

Alberto Bovone Titular Archbishop
of Caesarea in Numidia Secretary

Appendix Two

Notes

1. The expression "eastern methods" is used to refer to methods which are inspired by Hinduism and Buddhism, such as "Zen," "Transcendental Meditation," or "Yoga." Thus, it indicates methods of meditation of the non-Christian Far East which today are not infrequently adopted by some Christians also in their meditation. The orientation of the principles and methods contained in this present document is intended to serve as a reference point not just for this problem, but also, in a more general way, for the different forms of prayer practiced nowadays in ecclesial organizations, particularly in associations, movements, and groups.

2. Regarding the Book of Psalms in the prayer of the Church, cf. "Institutio generalis de Liturgia Horarum," nn. 100–109.

3. Cf. for example, Ex 15, Deut 32, 1 Sam 2, 2 Sam 22, and some prophetic texts, 1 Chron. 16.

4. Dogmatic Constitution "Dei Verbum," n. 2. This document offers other substantial indications for a theological and spiritual understanding of Christian prayer; see also, for example, nn. 3, 5, 8, 21.

5. Dogmatic Constitution "Dei Verbum," n. 25.

6. Regarding the prayer of Jesus, see "Institutio generalis de Liturgia Horarum," nn. 3–4.

7. Cf. "Institutio generalis de Liturgia Horarum," n. 9.

8. Pseudognosticism considered matter as something impure and degraded which enveloped the soul in an ignorance from which prayer had to free it, thereby raising it to true superior knowledge and so to a pure state. Of course not everyone was capable of this, only those who were truly spiritual; for simple believers, faith and observance of the commandments of Christ were sufficient.

9. The Messalians were already denounced by Saint Ephraim Syrus ("Hymni contra Haereses" 22, 4, ed. E. Beck, CSCO 169, 1957, p. 79) and later, among others, by Epiphanius of Salamina ("Panarion," also called "Adversus Haereses": PG 41, 156–1200; PG 42, 9–832), and Amphilochius, Bishop of Iconium ("Contra haereticos": G. Ficker, "Amphilochiana" I, Leipzig 1906, 21–77).

10. Cf., for example, St. John of the Cross, "Subida del Monte Carmelo," II, chap. 7. 11.

11. In the Middle Ages there existed extreme trends on the fringe of the Church. These were described not without irony, by one of the great Christian contemplatives, the Flemish Jan van Ruysbroek. He distinguished three types of deviations in the mystical life ("Die gheestelike Brulocht" 228. 12–230, 17: 230. 18- 32. 22: 232. 23–236. 6) and made a general critique of these forms (236, 7–237, 29). Similar techniques were subsequently identified and dismissed by St. Teresa of Avila who perceptively observed that "the very care taken not to

think about anything will arouse the mind to think a great deal," and that the separation of the mystery of Christ from Christian meditation is always a form of "betrayal" (see St. Teresa of Jesus. Vida 12, 5 and 22, 1–5).

12. Pope John Paul II has pointed out to the whole Church the example and the doctrine of St. Teresa of Avila who in her life had to reject the temptation of certain methods which proposed a leaving aside of the humanity of Christ in favor of a vague self-immersion in the abyss of the divinity. In a homily given on November 1, 1982, he said that the call of Teresa of Jesus advocating a prayer completely centered on Christ "is valid, even in our day, against some methods of prayer which are not inspired by the Gospel and which in practice tend to set Christ aside in preference for a mental void which makes no sense in Christianity. Any method of prayer is valid insofar as it is inspired by Christ and leads to Christ who is the Way, the Truth and the Life (cf. Jn. 14:6)." See: "Homilia Abulae habita in honorem Sanctae Teresiae:" AAS 75 (1983), 256–257.

13. See, for example, *The Cloud of Unknowing*, a spiritual work by an anonymous English writer of the fourteenth century.

14. In Buddhist religious texts, the concept of "Nirvana" is understood as a state of quiet consisting in the extinction of every tangible reality insofar as it is transient, and as such delusive and sorrowful.

15. Meister Eckhart speaks of an immersion "in the indeterminate abyss of the divinity" which is a "darkness in which the light of the Trinity never shines." Cf. "Sermo 'Ave Gratia Plena'" in fine (J. Quint, "Deutsche Predigten und Traktate" Hanser 1955, 261).

16. Cf. Pastoral Constitution "Gaudium et spes" n. 19, 1: "The dignity of man rests above all on the fact that he is called to communion with God. The invitation to converse with God is addressed to man as soon as he comes into being. For if man exists it is because God has created him through love, and through love continues to hold him in existence. He cannot live fully according to truth unless he freely acknowledges that love and entrusts himself to his creator."

17. As St. Thomas writes of the Eucharist: ". . . proprius effectus huius sacramenti est conversio) hominis in Christum ut dicat cum Apostolo: Vivo ego iam non ego; vivit vero in me Christus" (Gal 2:20)" (In IV Sent: d. 12, q. 2, a. 1).

18. Declaration "Nostra aetate" n. 2.

19. St. Ignatius of Loyola, "Ejercicios espirituales n. 23 et passim.

20. Cf. Col. 3:5: Rom. 6:11ff.: Gal. 5:24.

21. St. Augustine, *Enarrationes in Psalmos* XLI, 8: PL 36. 469.

22. St. Augustine, *Confessions* 3. 6. 11: PL 32, 688. Cf. "De vera Religione" 39. 72: PL 34, 154.

23. The positive Christian sense of the "emptying" of creatures stands out in an

exemplary way in St. Francis of Assisi. Precisely because he renounced creatures for love of God, he saw all things as being filled with his presence and resplendent in their dignity as God's creatures, and the secret hymn of their being is intoned by him in his "Cantico delle Creature." Cf. C. Esser, "Opuscula Sancti Patris Francisci Assisiensis" Ed. Ad Claras Aquas, Grottaferrata (Roma) 1978, pp. 83–86. In the same way he writes in the "Lettera a Tutti i Fedeli:" "Let every creature in heaven and on earth and in the sea and in the depth of the abyss (Rev. 5: 13) give praise, glory and honor and blessing to God, for he is our life and our strength. He who alone is good (Lk. 18: 19), who alone is the most high, who alone is omnipotent and admirable, glorious and holy, worthy of praise and blessed for infinite ages of ages. Amen" ("ibid Opuscula" 124). St. Bonaventure shows how in every creature Francis perceived the call of God and poured out his soul in the great hymn of thanksgiving and praise (cf. "Legenda S Francisci" chap. 9, n. 1, in "Opera Omnia" ed. Quaracchi 1898, Vol. VIII p 530).

24. See, for example, St. Justin, "Apologia" I 61, 12–13: PG 6 420–421: Clement of Alexandria, "Paedagogus" I, 6, 25–31: PG 8, 281–284; St. Basil of Caesarea, "Homiliae diversae" 13. 1: PG 31, 424– 425; St. Gregory Nazianzen, "Orationes" 40, 3, 1: PG 36, 361.

25. Dogmatic Constitution "Dei Verbum" n. 8.

26. The Eucharist, which the Dogmatic Constitution "Lumen Gentium" defines as "the source and summit of the Christian life" (LG 11), makes us "really share in the body of the Lord": in it "we are taken up into communion with him" (LG 7).

27. Cf. St. Teresa of Jesus, *Castillo Interior* IV 1, 2.

28. No one who prays, unless he receives a special grace, covets an overall vision of the revelations of God, such as St. Gregory recognized in St. Benedict, or that mystical impulse with which St. Francis of Assisi would contemplate God in all his creatures, or an equally global vision, such as that given to St. Ignatius at the River Cardoner and of which he said that for him it could have taken the place of Sacred Scripture. The "dark night" described by St. John of the Cross is part of his personal charism of prayer. Not every member of his order needs to experience it in the same way so as to reach that perfection of prayer to which God has called him.

29. The Christian's call to "mystical" experiences can include both what St. Thomas classified as a living experience of God via the gifts of the Holy Spirit and the inimitable forms (and for that reason forms to which one ought not to aspire) of the granting of grace. Cf. St. Thomas Aquinas, "Summa Theologiae" Ia, IIae, 1 c, as well as a. 5, ad 1.

30. See, for example, the early writers, who speak of the postures taken up by Christians while at prayer: Tertullian, "De Oratione" XIV PL 1 1170, XVII: PL I 1174–1176: Origen, "De Oratione" XXXI 2: PG 11, 550–553, and of the

meaning of such gestures; Barnabas, "Epistula" XII, 2–4: PG 2, 760–761: St. Justin, "Dialogus" 90, 4–5: PG 6, 689–692; St. Hippolytus of Rome, "Commentarium in Dan" III, 24: GCS I 168, 8–17; Origen, "Homiliae in Ex" XI 4: PG 12, 377–378. For the position of the body see also, Origen, "De Oratione" XXXI, 3: PG 11, 553–555.

31. Cf. St. Ignatius of Loyola, "Ejercicios Espirituales" n. 76.

32. Such as, for example, that of the Hesychast anchorites. Hesychia or external and internal quiet is regarded by the anchorites as a condition of prayer. In its oriental form it is characterized by solitude and techniques of recollection.

33. The practice of the "Jesus Prayer," which consists of repeating the formula, rich in biblical references, of invocation and supplication (e.g., "Lord Jesus Christ, Son of God, have mercy on me"), is adapted to the natural rhythm of breathing. In this regard, see St. Ignatius of Loyola, "Ejercicios Espirituales" n. 258.

34. Cf. 1 Thes. 5: 17, also 2 Thes. 3: 8–12. From these and other texts there arises the question of how to reconcile the duty to pray continually with that of working. See, among others, St. Augustine, "Epistula" 130, 20: PL 33, 501–502 and St. John Cassian, "De Institutis Coenobiorum" III, 1–3: SC 109, 92–93. Also, the "Demonstration of Prayer" by Aphraat, the first father of the Syriac Church, and in particular nn. 14–15, which deal with the so-called "works of Prayer" (cf. the edition of J. Parisot, "Afraatis Sapientis Persae Demonstrationes" IV PS 1, pp. 170–174).

35. Cf. St. Teresa of Jesus, *Castillo Interior* VII, 4, 6.

36. St. Augustine, "Enarrationes in Psalmos" CXLII 6: PL 37, 1849. Also see: St. Augustine, "Tract in Ioh." IV 9: PL 35, 1410: "Quando autem nec ad hoc dignum se dicit, vere plenus Spiritu Sancto erat, qui sic servus Dominum agnovit, et ex servo amicus fieri meruit."

ENDNOTES

1. J. Chryssavgis, *Soul Mending: The Art of Spiritual Direction* (Brookline, MA: Holy Cross Orthodox Press, 2000), 222.

2. Adolphe Tanquerey, *The Spiritual Life* (Rockford, IL: Tan, reprinted 2000 [original 1930]), no. 533 (De diversis, sermo VIII, 7).

3. Vincent Ferrer, *Treatise on the Spiritual Life* (Fitzwilliam, NH: Loreto Publications, 2006), 9.

4. Charles Hugo Doyle, *Guidance in Spiritual Direction* (New York: Roman Catholic Books, 1956), 8.

5. Blessed John Paul II, Apostolic Exhortation on the Vocation and the Mission of the Lay Faithful in the Church and in the World Christifideles Laici (December 30, 1988), no. 58.

6. Reginald Garragou-LaGrange, *The Three Ages of the Interior Life* (Rockford, IL: Tan 1989), 381.

7. Francis de Sales, *Introduction to the Devout Life* (New York: Doubleday, 2003), Part IV, Chapter 14 on Dryness and Spiritual Barrenness.

8. For more faithful perspective on the New Age and the Catholic Church, see Sharon Lee Giganti's website www.NewAgeDeception.com.

9. ENDOW: Educating on the Nature and Dignity of Women can be found at www.endowonline.org.

10. www.WalkingWithPurpose.com.

11. www.CSSProgram.net.

12. www.DisciplesofJesusandMary.org.

13. Chryssavgis, 207.

14. *The Priest, Minister of Divine Mercy* is available for download from the Congregation for the Clergy at http://www.clerus.org/english/news/00002638_The_priest__minister_of_divine_mercy___An_aid_for_confessors_and_spiritual_directors.html.

15. Classification of the soul refers to a means of understanding what phase of the spiritual life the directee is in, and thereby what the focus of spiritual direction should be. These classifications can be found in the section entitled, "The Three Ways of the Spiritual Life."

16. J. Chryssavgis, 180.

17. It is worth noting that there is disagreement between persons of good will regarding whether or not a director should charge for their services. The position of this book is not to advocate or argue for either approach but to focus on the heart of the directee.

18. St. Teresa of Avila, *The Book of Her Life, Collected Works of St. Teresa* (Washington: ICS Publications, 1987), vol. 1, ch. 6, sec. 8, p. 81.

19. *The Three Ages of the Interior Life*, Part 1, Chapter 6.

20. St. Louis De Montfort, *True Devotion to Mary* (Bay Shore, NY: Montfort Publications, 2006), 113–114.

21. Ibid., 106.

22. *Interior Castle*, Chapter 2.

23. *The Three Ages of the Interior Life*, Vol I, Part 2, Chapter 22.

24. Adapted from Ibid., 316-318.

25. Charles George Herbermann, *The Catholic Encyclopedia, An International Work of Reference on the Constitution, Doctrine,discipline, and History of the Catholic Church* (NY: The Encyclopedia Press, 1914), Vol 14, 254.

26. Eugene Boylan, *Difficulties in Mental Prayer* (Princeton, NJ: Scepter Press, 1997), 13.

27. *Interior Castle* (London: Thomas Baker, 1921) and http://www.sacred-texts.com/chr/tic/tic00.htm.

28. *The Collected Works of St. Teresa of Avila*, trans. Kieran Kavanaugh (Washington DC: Institute of Carmelite Studies, 1980), Volume II, 286.

29. Jean-Baptiste Chautard, *The Soul of the Apostolate* (Rockford: IL,1989),

177–179. Though Chautard encouraged classification of pilgrims in order to better help them in spiritual direction, this application of Chautard's categorization is unique to this book and the author is not aware of any similar efforts in Chautard's writings to align his own categorizations with the traditional three ways.

30. www.EWTN.com/devotions.

31. Note that though this level of maturity is still within the purgative stage, this is a significantly higher form of prayer than in the previous state and sometimes requires a great deal of time and energy to achieve, though God will ultimately decide how much progress is made regardless of the effort expended.

32. *The Collected Works of St. Teresa of Avila*, Volume II, Chapter 1, Paragraph 5.

33. Though St. Teresa does not use the language of the three ways, there is general consensus that her first three mansions reflect the realities of the purgative stage.

34. Translated and edited by E. Allison Peers From the Critical Edition of P. Silverio de Stanta Teresa, C.D. http://www.ewtn.com/library/spirit/castle.txt.

Are you looking to deepen your faith and relationship with God?

AVILA INSTITUTE

FOR SPIRITUAL FORMATION

The mission of the Avila Institute is to provide spiritual education and formation to Catholics around the world who are seeking to deepen their understanding and appropriation of the magisterium-faithful, mystical and ascetical patrimony of the Catholic Church.

With online instructors from around the country, the Avila Institute provides online instruction that cannot be found anywhere else!

www.Avila-Institute.com

Questions? Contact our Admissions Department:

admissions@myavila.com

NOTES

NOTES